MW01103627

digital
Dimensioning

digital
Dimensioning

Finding the Ebusiness in Your Business

Samuel C. Certo, Ph.D., and
Matthew W. Certo

McGraw-Hill
New York Chicago San Francisco Lisbon London Madrid
Mexico City Milan New Delhi San Juan Seoul
Singapore Sydney Toronto

Library of Congress Cataloging-in-Publication Data

Certo, Samuel C.
  Digital dimensioning: finding the ebusiness in your business / Samuel C. Certo,
Matthew W. Certo.
      p.   cm.
  Includes index.
  ISBN 0-07-137438-8
  1. Electronic commerce.   I. Certo, Matthew W. II. Title.
HF5548.32 .C468 2001
658.8'4—dc21

                                                                        2001030751

McGraw-Hill

A Division of The McGraw-Hill Companies

Copyright © 2001 by Samuel C. Certo and Matthew W. Certo. All rights reserved.
Printed in the United States of America. Except as permitted under the United States
Copyright Act of 1976, no part of this publication may be reproduced or distributed in
any form or by any means, or stored in a data base or retrieval system without the prior
written permission of the publisher.

1 2 3 4 5 6 7 8 9 0 AGM/AGM 0 9 8 7 6 5 4 3 2 1

ISBN 0-07-137438-8

This book was set in Garamond by MM Design 2000, Inc.

Printed and bound by Quebecor World/Martinsburg.

McGraw-Hill books are available at special quantity discounts to use as premiums and
sales promotions, or for use in corporate training programs. For more information,
please write to the Director of Special Sales, Professional Publishing, McGraw-Hill, Two
Penn Plaza, New York, NY 10121-2298. Or contact your local bookstore.

 This book is printed on recycled, acid-free paper containing a minimum of 50%
recycled, de-inked fiber.

In memory of Salvatore Certo—father and grandfather—whose entrepreneurial endeavors in the old economy serve as both lessons and inspirations to those of us striving in the new economy.

—SCC & MWC

Contents

Preface

In the beginning it all seemed so simple. Put a product on the Web and a swell of orders would surely follow. Better yet, write a business plan one week and do an IPO the next. It was hard not to get caught up in the excitement. After all, a revolution of historical proportion was unfolding. Do you remember where you were when Netscape went public? Gen-Xers talk about that milestone like Baby Boomers lament the Kennedy assassination.

Not only did it seem simple, but it was happening fast—really fast. While old-line companies were scratching their heads in bewilderment, young start-ups were scrambling to get started and beat others to the punch. Along the way, it became fashionable to spend money. And lots of it. Multimillion-dollar launch parties, BMW employment incentives, and lavish corporate offices (often mistaken for palaces) became standard fare. And then reality set in. After spending and spending, companies started to run out of money. It became strikingly obvious that brand equity could be bought during halftime of the Super Bowl, but brand equity wouldn't go very far when it was time to meet the payroll. Dotcom start-ups began to fail.

At the same time, others have come to enjoy tremendous successes. Both start-ups and traditional companies have succeeded by applying the promising tools of Internet business to their organizations. In many cases, consumer lives have been improved, jobs have been created, and progress has been witnessed.

The purpose of this book is to explain the delineation between ebusiness failures and successes and guide managers toward the latter. The ideas and concepts contained herein have been germinating for a number of years, sparked during client engagements and over countless cups of coffee. We have seen successes and failures of organizations large and small against the dynamic backdrop of the new economy. This book is the synthesis of our observations and conclusions as validated in organizations around the world.

Our approach in explaining these practices and concepts is a diversion from other books concerning new-economy trends. Since our intent is to clearly present practical steps toward achieving ebusiness success, the book's structure is more learning-oriented and less hype-oriented. Our book does not bombard users with ethereal terms or buzzwords like *business transformation* or *organizational reinvention*. While we acknowledge the magnitude of change introduced by ebusiness opportunities, our intent is to educate managers on practical remedies and tactics. Our focus is one of simplicity and practicality—not melodrama and frenzy.

Through all the lavish launch parties, industry prophecy, and dotcom hype, one notion has faded into the background: From the multinational conglomerate headquartered in a building in Manhattan to the hot dog vendor located just outside, organizations must satisfy customers while generating a profit. Ebusiness efforts should be helping organizations to achieve this bellwether goal—not detracting their attention from it. Digital dimensioning is a process whose fundamental purpose is to bring this concept back to the forefront.

The format of the book is unique. As individual topics are presented in each chapter, several tools are included to reinforce concepts. Chapters begin with Executive Previews to introduce their overall direction. Each chapter also contains a Spotlight feature to introduce a core concept as seen in an actual organizational environment. In each of these chapter Spotlights, actual case studies connect theoretical content to practical examples. Next, the core theory of a chapter is presented. Immediately following chapter theory, the case study is concluded to relate a consultant's perspective on the subject company's situation and proposed action. The last component of each chapter is a list titled "Digital Dimensioning Resolutions." This list contains key points designed to help managers summarize content and immediately implement theories in their present-day organizational circumstances.

A further tool for facilitating a truly enriching experience is the book's companion Web site, located online at http://www.digital-dimensioning.com. From the standpoint of personal development, this Web site includes self-teaching exercises based upon concepts presented in each chapter. Additionally, the site includes links to related chapter resources, daily content related to book material, and background information on the authors. From the perspective of collaborative learning, the site facilitates community interaction on book concepts and relevant current issues. Presented in a useful and engaging format, the companion Web site should be considered an integral component of the digital dimensioning process.

Acknowledgments

Our excitement in publishing a book of this nature is indescribable. The opportunity to discuss our ideas about the revolutionary digital business age in a worldwide forum is simply exhilarating.

As with the development of any book, however, our book is the result of the efforts and commitment of many different people. This section is certainly one of our favorite parts of our book because we can give credit where credit is due.

First, and perhaps foremost, our colleagues at WebSolvers have played a very special role in the development of this book. Their support and encouragement during the project have been vital to its completion. Witnessing their commitment to the growth and success of the organization has inspired our writing. In particular, we would like to thank Jeff Owens, whose dedication to our company continues to impress us daily; Anne Simmons, whose aggressiveness fuels our growth; Deborah Westgate, who perpetually contributes to our positive culture; and Cheryl Johnson, who serves as a cornerstone and pillar of our operations.

In addition, both the trust and the support of the clients at Web-Solvers have been invaluable. Their confidence in our ideas and their willingness to apply them have provided validation for digital dimensioning concepts. The tough-mindedness and diligent focus of our clients on the success of their own organizations have been a constant reminder that digital impact on organizations must make good business sense.

For both Sam and Matt Certo, Rollins College has been very instrumental in the development of this book. From Sam Certo as a faculty member, special recognition goes to the Crummer Graduate School of

Business. In essence, the school is a catalyst for generating new business ideas. Over the years, the Crummer "family" has vigilantly focused on formulating and disseminating ideas that practicing businesspeople can apply and MBA students can use to accelerate their success. The school's recently developed emphasis on ebusiness has been a vivid and constant reminder of the education and research that needs to be tailored for the new digital arena. The students at Crummer have also helped to develop this book. Their questioning and natural curiosity have provided a continual debate and refinement of the tenets of this book.

From Matt Certo's alumnus perspective on Rollins, thanks and appreciation go to the many faculty and staff who have supported and encouraged him in his quest to participate in the cultural revolution that is the Internet. Mr. Les Lloyd, Assistant Vice President of Information Technology, has been both a guide and beacon in the world of technology and management. Ms. Cynthia Wood, Associate Vice President of Alumni Relations, has been both a supporter and encourager since day one. Mr. Larry Humes, Associate Vice President of Public Relations, has gone the extra mile time and time again to help a student learn in countless ways. Collective thanks is owed to the entire Rollins College Alumni Association, whose commitment to the growth of students and the campus has paved the way for the success of many.

Both Certos would like to give special thanks to Rita Bornstein, president of Rollins College, for maintaining an educational climate in which new ideas can be conceived and developed in an atmosphere of mutual support and encouragement. Dr. Bornstein's personal support and encouragement have been a significant lift personally and professionally. She truly embodies Rollins's commitment to education, community, and service.

Naturally, the contributions of our reviewers must not go unnoticed. These individuals have shared insights about the relevance of digital dimensioning and have helped us to develop an approach to this book that emphasizes both pragmatism and the building of company value through digital applications. Our reviewers—Rick Goings, Chairman and CEO, Tupperware Corporation; Deanne Gabel, General Manager, Disney Institute; James Suskiewich, Chairman/Chief Executive Officer, Federal Trust Corporation; Philip B. Crosby, Chairman and CEO, Philip Crosby Associates II, Inc.; Bradley L. Rozema, Vice President, Merrill Lynch—have been fantastic. Simply put, their comments on the manuscript have been invaluable.

We have been fortunate indeed to have the support of McGraw-Hill, a world-renowned publisher, throughout the development of this book. For any organization, people build its reputation for excellence. McGraw-Hill is no exception. Michelle Williams, our editor, has provided global insights about publishing as well as more focused advice on publishing about ebusiness. Michelle's support and encouragement throughout this project were invaluable. Undoubtedly, without Michelle there would be no book. Janice Race, our editing supervisor, played a vital part in fine-tuning the manuscript. In addition, other members of the McGraw-Hill production, marketing, and publicity teams have provided critical support. Special thanks to Andy Winston, Acquisitions Editor, McGraw-Hill/Irwin, for encouragement and support throughout the conceptualization and writing of this project.

Members of the Certo family are a continual encouragement to one another. We would like to thank the rest of our family for the support shown throughout the development of this book. Mimi, the matriarch of the family, displayed a constant tenderness and warmth that helped to overcome challenges. Brian contributed exuberance that helped us to remember that all things are possible. Sarah inspired tenacity that helped us to maintain focus throughout the project. Trevis and Missy contributed Skylar, the newest member of the Certo family. Skylar reminded us why we do projects of this nature—for future generations.

Lastly, we'd like to thank God, without whose blessings it would be impossible for us to participate in projects of this nature.

Samuel C. Certo
Matthew W. Certo

chapter 1

The Exciting World of Ebusiness

Executive Preview

This chapter's fundamental purpose is to introduce the concept of *digital dimensioning* and demonstrate its value as a vital component in the process of achieving organizational success. Digital dimensioning describes the evolution of a new, faster pace of business wrought by heightened competition and high financial rewards. The chapter explains how much of this behavior has been based upon new business assumptions created by fierce competition, popularized by industry attitudes, and accentuated by mainstream media. As a result of business approaches based upon these assumptions, many organizations have suffered negative and in some cases fatal economic consequences. The chapter concludes with a brief introduction to digital dimensioning as a core management philosophy that acknowledges the new considerations of the Internet and other electronic technologies and guides managers toward organizational success in light of the challenges of this brave new world.

Business at Internet Speed

On August 9, 1995, the stock market opened at 9:30 a.m., just like any other Wednesday. Microsoft shares opened slightly lower, while the stock of Coca-Cola surged to an all-time high. But neither of these blue-chip stories got much attention on this summer day. Instead, a young software company that was making its debut on the NASDAQ dominated most of the financial headlines.

The company's stock, which had opened at $28 per share, quickly screamed to $74.25 before finally settling at $58.25 at the market's close. Its founder, a 23-year-old software programmer just 2 years out of college, had seen his software idea rapidly evolve from a dorm-room brainchild into Wall Street's latest success story. By 4:30 p.m. that day, Marc Andreessen, key architect of Netscape Communications, had seen his net worth rise to nearly $80 million. Just months earlier, his job as a part-time computer programmer for his college had paid him a mere $6.85 per hour. However, stories like Andreessen's in 1995 are in stark contrast to many others of 2000. Impatient investors and flawed business models forced many Internet ventures to lay off workers, cut spending drastically, and in some cases discontinue operations altogether. The freewheeling headlines of the mid-to-late nineties were quickly replaced by stories of tearful executives breaking bad news to employees. Managers of both start-ups and corporate Internet initiatives began to rethink their approaches altogether. The beginning of dotcom mania, though, set the tone for many things to come. While many stories have had sad endings, the energy and fervor of companies like Netscape built a tremendous amount of momentum behind a business revolution. Digital dimensioning is a process and operational philosophy designed to help managers guide their organizations toward ultimate success using the momentum that sparked the revolution, yet exercising the caution and discipline that many failures have lacked.

Many have heard the story of Andreessen and Netscape, but few recognize its significance as an industrial milestone. The Netscape initial public offering was unique in several ways. First of all, the founder was abnormally young. Typically, founding participants in successful IPOs had been seasoned industry executives with a wealth of managerial experience—not recent college graduates with virtually no business background. Second, it was peculiar to see a stock price climb 165 percent during its first day of trading. Most companies are delighted to see 10 to 15 percent rises in market capitalization on the first day of trading. Third, Netscape had yet to turn a profit. According to its IPO prospectus, the firm had lost $8.5 million during 1994 and was on track for comparable 1995 losses at the time of the offering. Most investors typically looked for a record of strong earnings growth as a fundamental prerequisite for investment; this was obviously an exception given the high demand for Netscape stock during its first day of trading.

But perhaps the most unique aspect of all was that Netscape's core business—consumer and commercial Internet software—depended and capitalized on the commercial opportunities of the Internet. At the time, most businesses and investors were just beginning to seriously consider that the Internet could bring about a mainstay revolution in commerce. Those in the investment community were speculating that companies in a position to capitalize on the revolution would yield high financial rewards. The Netscape offering, among the earliest "Internet IPOs," confirmed this position.

Because of its unique circumstances, the runaway initial public offering of Internet start-up Netscape quickly set a new overall tone in the investment community. Specifically, investors would handsomely reward founders of Internet companies pursuing an exciting idea even if management was inexperienced and earnings were nonexistent. In fact, many companies had not only a long history of losses, but a lack of foreseeable or even projected future earnings. Investors' threshold for risk was rising in light of the Internet's astounding commercial potential.

It didn't take long for the tone to resonate to entrepreneurs in similar circumstances. All across the United States, groups of would-be entrepreneurs and teams of corporate strategists began to develop strategies for start-ups designed to take advantage of the overwhelming financial opportunities. If it were possible for a college student with virtually no business experience to generate an idea and be on the front page of the *Wall Street Journal* in just a matter of months, the opportunity for others seemed well within reach. What quickly followed was an epidemic of start-up companies with diverse business models and names ending in ".com."

With all the excitement came an incredible sense of urgency to execute quickly. Some start-ups rushed to be the first within their industry groups to hit the stock exchanges, assuming that the first to market would be perceived as the front-runner. Others feared that competitive pressures would be too overwhelming unless the capital acquired by a public offering became accessible very soon. Still, other start-ups felt pressure to quickly enter the public marketplace, fearing that the investor euphoria driving successful offerings would subside or cease altogether. While many headlines and articles validated and even perpetuated the liberal IPO environment, others speculated about how long the somewhat abnormal investment behavior would last. Whatever the case, the general pressure to move fast was extremely high. Multitudes of start-ups were evolving at various stages and approaching the investment community in droves. Inside larger corporations, management began looking for ways to use the Internet to build deeper relationships with suppliers as a way to increase margins. New industries like eprocurement began to evolve quickly because of the Internet's ability to automate rudimentary processes. Online exchanges addressed the needs of entire industries—from supplier and distributor to retailer and consumer—and offered efficiencies and opportunities to all the players. The Internet frenzy had arrived.

The magnitude of this pressure drove many founding employees to abnormal lengths to move quickly. The underlying motto called for entering markets first at any expense. In an effort to do just that, stories of sacrifice and reprioritized lives were typical of early Internet start-ups. It was not uncommon for employees to work 100 or more hours per week during a company's first several months. In pursuit of tremendous wealth, many gave up normal lives and routines and replaced them with unorthodox concessions. More often than not, many of these behaviors revolved around accomplishing something in a short amount of time in order to outmaneuver would-be competitors.

There are countless legends and stories of company founders going to extremes to do so. Some resorted to sleeping in offices for weeks at a time in an effort to meet a pressing developmental deadline. Some Internet start-ups such as Tellme.com installed bunk beds in offices for those employees who would work well into the night and needed a place to sleep between shifts. Not having the "luxury" of in-office bunk beds, Yahoo cofounder David Filo even slept under his desk during the early days of his company's growth. Others commuted thousands of miles to their jobs weekly for the opportunity to work with promising start-ups. Subsequently, family and personal lives of start-up employees took a back seat with the hope that sacrifices in the present could possibly yield astronomic financial rewards in the future. Still, others abandoned steady jobs and committed lifetime savings to finance a personal business vision. The financial windfalls of Andreessen and others have been so huge that followers have been willing to risk nearly everything on the hope of being the next headline story.

While many influenced by the likes of young Wall Street successes have been start-up companies, equally eager to embrace the potential rewards of the Internet have been the world's most established and fortified companies. Companies that have been in business for several decades recognize that the digital revolution presents both opportunities for new market positions and threats against existing ones. Subsequently, the tone of corporate boardrooms has changed from that of complacency to that of defense and aggression. The same financial opportunities and competitive pressures that have motivated start-ups to move quickly are pushing established companies to react swiftly as well. The pace at which opportunities and threats emerge to both established companies and industries has been furious. Online retailers, for example, have emerged to apply enormous competitive pressure on the world's most established traditional retailers by providing in-home convenience and rock-bottom pricing. To react, traditional retailers have developed and executed a variety of strategies designed to take advantage of Internet excitement and pressure. Met with a new set of challenges and opportunities, they consider a variety of alternatives as vehicles to move forward. While there are a number of different possibilities in doing so, most have chosen one of three basic models for capitalizing on the advantages of the online retail environment. The three approaches at the disposal of managers are spin-offs, strategic partnerships, and internal business units. Table 1.1 depicts these three options available to managers.

Table 1.1 Traditional retailers commonly use one of three models to take advantage of online retailing opportunities.

Model	Spin-Off	Strategic Partnership	Internal Business Unit
Examples	barnesandnoble.com Expedia	RiteAid Drugstore.com	Gap Nike
Characteristics	New separate company independent of parent	Separate existing companies	New operating unit managed by parent

Spin-Offs

The first choice is to create a separate company to concentrate on Internet opportunities. Many have incubated separate businesses (or spin-offs) specifically for online activity. Barnes & Noble, one of the world's leading booksellers, formed a separate company called barnesandnoble.com to focus solely on online retail. The new company successfully completed an IPO to independently finance the venture; the capital raised in the offering is helping barnesandnoble.com to invest in Internet growth opportunities.

Spin-offs are typically owned by the parent company but operate autonomously. There is often interaction and cooperation with the parent company while maintaining independent management, policies, and procedures. While spin-off companies do lose some benefit of the parent's established infrastructure, they gain the energy and enthusiasm that comes with starting a brand-new business. Many public companies have chosen this route because the large start-up expenses required in internally incubating such an endeavor can seriously hurt the parent company's financial statements. In addition, the spin-off itself creates a vehicle to raise start-up and operational capital through the investment marketplace.

Strategic Partnerships

Deterred by the magnitude of commitment involved in starting a spin-off company, other traditional retailers have taken different approaches to capitalizing on Internet opportunities. The second common approach involves partnering with an online company. Traditional pharmacy RiteAid, for example, formed a strategic partnership with online pharmacy drugstore.com. In addition to being marketing partners, the two companies collaboratively assist customers who want to shop online yet need the services of a traditional store. These include same-day prescription fulfillment and pharmacist assistance. Similarly, drugstore.com customers can return or exchange merchandise in RiteAid retail outlets. Customers have the in-home conveniences from online outlets coupled with the same-day services of traditional retail stores. In strategic partnerships such as the one between RiteAid and drugstore.com, financial gain can be realized for both through revenue sharing or licensing fees.

The benefits of partnership in this fashion are many. First of all, both strategic partners have immediate access to the other's customer base and operational infrastructure. This prevents the partners from having to independently procure resources or endure the lengthy time frames of doing so. Second, neither partner assumes overwhelming financial risk in creating an alternate presence. For example, RiteAid does not have to invest a tremendous amount of resources to have an online presence that adequately serves customers. Likewise, drugstore.com does not need to invest in building an extensive network of physical locations to serve customer with in-store needs.

Strategic partnerships do have potential pitfalls, however. Most importantly, it is difficult to attain much control over processes or practices when each partner is under separate management. To a great extent, each strategic partner must rely on the other's judgment in meeting the needs of customers. Further, the partners must operate cooperatively in the face of possible conflict. For example, if drugstore.com begins to develop a reputation for sluggish order fulfillment, RiteAid runs the risk of being associated with these negative customer opinions. For many traditional retailers, though, strategic partnerships are a relatively safe and easy route to entering the online arena without enduring the more involved spin-off process.

Internal Business Units

Still, other traditional retailers have taken a third approach to entering the online marketplace. Instead of forming a new company or partnering with an existing one, they have created internal business units that are integral to the company's traditional operations. The Gap, one of the world's leading clothing and fashion retailers with over 3400 stores globally, has simply developed an internal business unit to exploit online opportunities that exist as a result of the company's traditional stature and brand. In this instance, the company's traditional management maintains total control of its online efforts and can utilize the existing operational infrastructure of the parent corporation. Unlike those of spin-offs, managers of internal business units do not have to endure the establishment and development of new technology and human resources infrastructure. At the same time, many internal business units never realize their full potential because of mandates and political constraints of the parent corporation that are inconsistent with the best practices of online business.

Whether through spin-offs, strategic partnerships, or internal business units, traditional companies are exploring different avenues toward defending existing market positions or pursuing new growth opportunities brought about by the advent of digital technology. Traditional corporations must explore available alternatives for online involvement and select the one that seems most appropriate. While there are several variations for doing so, spin-offs, strategic partnerships, and internal business units are the most popular and viable.

Various alternatives for approaching Internet business opportunities have certainly affected the retail shopping industry in a relatively short period of time. There are cases where the Internet's impact has been felt almost immediately. The record industry—one with both business to consumer (B2C) and business to business (B2B) implications—is one example. Over several decades, music publishing evolved to be the primary point of connection and distribution between artists and consumers. As a result, major record labels have traditionally held all the cards in terms of which bands receive recording contracts, which songs are released to radio stations, and which albums are distributed to record retailers. In 1998, however, the advent of MP3 technology began to erode the solidified position of record companies. This new digital music format allowed artists to digitally encode their work and send it to interested consumers, thereby circumventing record companies altogether. Soon after, the birth of Napster brought the record industry to its knees within a matter of weeks. Shawn Fanning, the creator of Napster, had built a freely downloadable piece of Internet software that allowed music lovers to share their favorite MP3 songs with others around the world. The software package grew primarily by word of mouth beginning in 1999. From February to August 2000, the number of unique users grew from 1.1 million to 6.7 million, an increase of over 500 percent. By the end of 2000, Napster had over 38 million users. Instead of going to record stores to buy music, consumers began looking to Napster for their favorite songs and avoiding the stores altogether. In just a matter of weeks, a relatively simple piece of software that was created in a dorm room had dealt a powerful, almost paralyzing, blow to a century-old industry. That's the nature of the Internet.

These factors of high rewards, competitive pressure, and threats to established positions have created an environment of pure speed. The media and their subjects use buzzwords such as *time to market, category killer*, and *transformation* to describe this new landscape of high competition, high speed, and high risk. Many companies have used the notion of speed to create a sense of urgency and spur a call to action. iXL, a company that builds Internet solutions like Web sites for corporations, has used emphatic verbiage on its home page to motivate clients to develop and implement strategies quickly:

> Blink. A "dot-com" company is after your market. Click. Your customers are buying online right now. Bang! The starting gun for transforming your business has been fired.

By describing the fast pace of Internet competition, iXL is emphasizing the competitive pressures inherent in this new business environment and conveying the need to move quickly in order to achieve success. Many often refer to the high pace at which online initiatives are evolving as "Internet speed." Some have even proclaimed that since so many are moving with such urgency, time lines of online businesses should be referenced in terms of "Internet years." Similar to the timetable used for household pets, 1 year according to a traditional calendar is equivalent to several years in Internet years. While the fierce pace of the Internet has propelled many to astronomical success, it has likely hurt more than it has helped. Many organizations have failed drastically, primarily because of trying to grow or evolve too quickly. The dotcom decline that began in 2000 claimed many victims for this reason alone. Consequently, the behavior of many entrepreneurs and managers has fallen in line with the popularization of this operating environment. The changes in behavior, primarily, have been most clearly seen in the objectives upon which managers focus. The media have glorified early-stage financing, successful initial public offerings, and exponential sales growth. As a result, many executives have established these as primary business objectives.

The difficulty with this approach, however, is that these objectives are not always appropriate for the circumstances of every organization. Irregularly high sales growth, for example, can be a negative circumstance when the cost of those sales to the organization far outweighs the resultant revenues. Additionally, being overly committed to appeasing private or public investors is unhealthy when it distracts management's attention from satisfying the organization's internal and external customers. Undoubtedly, sales growth and successful commercial financing are critical to a growing organization's success. When factors such as these detract from core objectives of profitability and customer satisfaction, though, the prospects of an organization's long-term success are significantly diminished.

None of this is to say that those aggressively driving this environment of speed are not admirable. Quite the contrary. It is commonly held that the increased speed and efficiency at which many companies are growing and operating has been predominantly responsible for the economic boom in the latter part of the twentieth century. The Internet frenzy has created new jobs and significant private and public investment in new venture development. But the high speed at which *some* companies have succeeded, coupled with the fact that many have prospered in spite of overwhelming odds, has created a set of false assumptions upon which many start-ups and spin-offs are now initiated.

False Assumptions of the New Economy

When start-up successes are glorified—usually following some milestone of success like an IPO—most of what's discussed and written about is the original idea and the financial windfall that ultimately followed. What sometimes goes unmentioned is the description of iterative financing that carried the company to that milestone. Angel financing followed by multitiered venture capital supplemented by bridge debt financing leads to eventual financial viability. Each of these financing events (or rounds) involves the financial risk of one or more parties at multiple points in time. In many instances, the failure to secure capital during any one of these stages might result in the firm's financial doom. Many companies have been fortunate enough to acquire the appropriate capital during critical junctures and aggressively move forward with operations. Given this notion, some entrepreneurs *assume* that capital will be readily available all along their path as well. They also *assume* that the firm's original investors will be forever loyal to the founders and therefore contribute more capital as it becomes needed. But when unreasonable rates of growth force firms to burn more capital than is available and investors refuse to contribute further, some firms are forced to discontinue operations. It is important that management not depend solely on the acquisition of more capital in the event that it is not available. This and some other false assumptions along with actual realities are contained in Table 1.2.

Investor dependence is not the only dangerous assumption made by growing companies. Others falsely place their faith in customer loyalty. Many of the firms that are trying to grow quickly do so by investing heavily in customer acquisition. Splashy television ads during the Super Bowl and multipage layouts in leading national periodicals were mainstays of the early dotcom years. Super Bowls during the beginning of

Table 1.2 Many of the commonly held assumptions of the new economy have somewhat conflicting realities.

Assumption	Reality
The customers we paid to acquire today will be ours tomorrow because we were the first to serve them.	With little or no human content involved in a transaction, customers we acquire today will gravitate toward the online vendor with the lowest prices tomorrow.
If we burn through investment capital too fast, our investors will contribute more to finance our continuing operations.	If we burn through investment capital too fast, it's possible that we will be unable to secure additional capital to continue operating.
Whoever secures the most market share initially will be the long-term winner in any segment.	The long-term winner in any market segment depends upon successful execution over the long-term, not just the early stages.
An initial public offering is a necessary step in growing a successful company	An initial public offering is a business tool that is not appropriate for all companies

the Internet frenzy were dominated by dotcom players. More recent Super Bowls, however, were noticeably devoid of Internet advertisements, giving way to more traditional advertisers like Pepsi. The general mentality at that time was to invest enormous amounts of start-up capital to acquire customers and build market share through advertising and sales promotion. Many assume that paying handsomely to acquire customers now will translate into retained market share in the future: "If we're the ones to serve them first, they'll be around forever." But there is a fundamental problem with this strategy in that customer loyalty online is a rickety foundation upon which to build long-term operational philosophy. Traditionally, loyalty between consumers and retailers has not grown from brand awareness alone. It has grown, rather, from the personal relationships between consumers and the individual company representatives with whom they deal.

In face-to-face transactions conducted with traditional retailers in which customers repeatedly purchase goods and services with the help of one or more individuals, relationships begin to develop between buyer and seller. At these times, buyer and seller sometimes talk about respective family members, personal hobbies, or current events. Buyers begin to prefer particular vendors based upon the intangible value and benefit of these relationships. In many cases, buyers develop strong loyalty toward the person who has served them repeatedly. Even if there is a problem with a transaction, the value of the personal relationship sometimes outweighs the negative issue.

In many cases, customers feel indebted to the individual and are unwilling to switch vendors because of the potential strain this might inflict on the personal relationship. One episode of the popularized television show *Seinfeld* illustrates this concept as it exists in our culture. When the show's main character, Jerry Seinfeld, grows terribly dissatisfied with his barber and friend Enzo of several years, he hesitates in switching barbers because of how upset Enzo would be. Jerry secretly arranges for Enzo's partner Gino to cut his hair without Enzo knowing. The episode comically portrays the switch in the light of having a love affair behind the back of a current partner. This Seinfeld illustration certainly goes beyond the norm in portraying customer loyalty, but the point is reflective of a very tangible selling component. In commercial transactions made by consumers, loyalty grows from the personal relationships that result from repeated face-to-face contact over a period of time. For sellers, this becomes a means of building long-term clientele.

Consumers' loyalty to sales and customer service representatives can begin to supersede price as the primary factor in a purchase decision. The customer begins to assign value to the personal relationships inherent in transactions. This is precisely why so many sales coaches and managers strongly emphasize the notion of customer relationship building.

In ecommerce transactions, however, the opportunity for personal relationship building is severely diminished. The most commercially rewarding aspect of ecommerce is, in turn, perhaps its greatest potential threat. By removing the human element from the sales process, price becomes a stronger factor in influencing a customer's decision. In an Internet transaction, there is no "small talk" between buyer and seller, no personal strings attached to the transaction. However, several developments in Web site architecture and infrastructure are attempting to address this issue. Several Internet applications allow customers to interact with site representatives in real-time via text or voice chat. Some sites utilize shopping assistants who actually "accompany" a user through a site and offer advice and feedback on products. While many of these technologies are expected to make online experiences more personal, few expect their impact to fully supplant actual in-person interaction.

In this context, it is more challenging to build loyalty and almost impossible to instill the guilt that Jerry Seinfeld felt. There are certainly other ways to create intangible value within transactions. Amazon.com has clearly mastered the art of ordering convenience with its patented "1-Click" ordering system. But issues such as ordering convenience can quickly become commoditized by the creation of similar ordering processes by competitive online stores. Ultimately, this is bad news for organizations that pay high prices to acquire consumers quickly, because future price pressure can just as quickly erode leading positions in market share.

The customer loyalty assumption is a dangerous one. A description of typical start-up expense cycles coupled with a picture of assumed *and* realistic revenue cycles shows the potential danger of unrealistic loyalty expectations. When a new Internet company conceptualizes a new product or service offering, it generally endures two kinds of expenses when entering the marketplace. The first category, start-up costs, comprises one-time expenses involved in building the company's initial infrastructure, developing the first iteration of its product, and acquiring customers through high-reach advertising. While start-up expenses are normally very high, they no longer exist once a business has established its base infrastructure.

The second classification, operating expenses, is made up of those recurring expenses such as salaries and rent which are necessary to the company's current and future ongoing operations. While they are not typically as high as start-up expenses, they normally rise over the course of a business's life span and exist as long as a company is in business. Each type of expense has a normal cycle of growth or decline. But since both are indeed expenses and/or significant cash outflows, it is important to appreciate the collective impact of the two.

Most companies anticipate that the cash outflows involved in start-up expenses will produce residual revenues that come from successful advertising and subsequent customer acquisition. In essence, many start-ups assume that paying the high price of acquiring customers initially will generate significant revenue eventually because the customers did business with the organization. Realistically, though, today's online customers, lacking the loyalty ties of traditional retail, will likely migrate to lower-cost retailers tomorrow. This presents a financial dilemma for online companies that hope to recover customer acquisition costs from the future revenues of their association.

The origin of these false assumptions is curious. Some Internet companies have indeed succeeded by growing market share at an astronomical pace. Likewise, many Internet companies have gone through several rounds of financing to fund continued growth. These stories have been glorified in the popular press along with the Marc Andreessen success sagas. But all these examples culminate into the largest assumption of all: that one company's road map for growth can be applied to the next. On the contrary, factors of timing, market maturity, and investor sentiment make the success factors of Internet business opportunities very different. What worked then will not necessarily work now.

Moreover, managers of emerging enterprises have begun to use the popular press as a measuring stick for Internet success. Consumer periodicals and television programs have profiled Internet start-ups and Fortune 500 Web efforts that are engaging in aggressive growth practices while assuming enormous financial risks on behalf of public and private investors. These stories are certainly newsworthy because of their unique characteristics. But many have sensed the aspects of glamour that come with this media attention and have followed suit in pursuit of the potential rewards. Following the demise of several Internet initiatives, this factor has been tempered significantly by the realities of layoffs and lost fortunes.

The Continuum of Ebusiness Success

Unfortunately, companies that receive splashy press coverage are not necessarily being profiled because of their economic success. Many times, instead, they are being chronicled because of their unconventional approach to spending with little or no calculated projection for return on investment. Perhaps inaccurately, these companies are profiled in the light of success and aggressiveness instead of a risky and unrealistic light. Managers with aspirations for ebusiness success run the risk of long-term failure if they project and measure their own success according to these "success stories."

Gauging ebusiness success must be done according to more conventional standards for organizational health. A company that spends millions of dollars on a Super Bowl advertisement is not necessarily successful but perhaps overly risk-tolerant. When such risks yield little rewards, organizations have three fundamental choices to recover: Either scale back operational expenses through personnel layoffs, raise more capital to finance future operations, or do some combination of the two. Failure to properly execute one of these alternatives could ultimately lead to organizational death by insolvency.

Many of the most exciting, original Internet start-ups experienced this general set of circumstances not long after the IPO boom of the late 1990s. In fiscal year 2000, just a few short years after a long run of sky-rocketing Internet IPOs, reality began to set in. Investors initially willing to tolerate high risk in the face of absent earnings began to waiver. Internet company stock prices that briefly hovered between $50 and $60 plummeted to below $10. Some fell below $2 per share, prompting delisting warnings from the NASDAQ stock exchange. Others, including Drkoop.com and CDNOW, received letters from their independent auditing firms explaining that their current financial situation was potentially fatal and that financial adjustments needed to be made. Only time will tell if such adjustments will contribute to ultimate success.

In all the excitement to grow quickly, many companies became insolvent, a formal economic term for running out of money. In many instances of insolvency, management has been put in a position in which it must devote more attention to raising operational capital, naturally diverting attention from the satisfaction of customers. While these companies have surely fallen upon adverse circumstances, there is still the continuing possibility that changes in strategic direction supplemented by fresh capital could realistically result in ultimate success. Because it is often premature to label financially struggling Internet businesses as commercial failures, an appropriate classification is that of *ebusiness defenders* because of the defensive posture assumed as a result of these dire circumstances.

For other firms, the results have been much more severe. Many have experienced such drastic financial consequences of mismanaged growth that they have been forced to discontinue their operations. Quite simply, their total cost curve has far outpaced the corresponding revenue curve leading to realized insolvency or organizational death. Early examples of insolvent Internet companies include pets.com, living.com, and homewarehouse.com. While swift movement to market is critical to establishing an early competitive edge, these firms are a reminder that unless managed properly, Internet speed can kill. In the context of this book, *ebusiness failures* will be used to characterize those commercial Internet initiatives that were voluntarily or involuntarily terminated due to improperly managed finances or growth. Other organizations have been notable in achieving success using ebusiness practices. While success in itself can be defined to varying degrees, *ebusiness successes* are defined as those organizations that have achieved vital objectives (positive earnings growth, positive cashflow, and increased shareholder value) through an appropriate use of electronic management tools. Certainly, successes of today can unfortunately become failures of tomorrow due to a host of circumstances and management decisions. For this reason, *ebusiness success* is an appropriate characterization only when the organization displays trends—not merely instances—of vital objective achievement.

While other organizations have yet to demonstrate trends in achieving vital objectives using ebusiness tools, they have displayed sporadic instances. At the same time, their positions in the marketplace show strong promise, with some unresolved exceptions. But since their financial position is likely better than that of *ebusiness defenders*, their classification is more positive. These firms are characterized as *ebusiness cultivators* since their use of ebusiness activities directed toward objective achievement is positively developing. Along the continuum, their positions are less developed than those of *ebusiness successes* because of unresolved or immature marketplace circumstances. Table 1.3 portrays some examples of various companies that hold positions along this continuum.

Table 1.3 Ebusiness success should be gauged by tangible factors, not media or industry glorification.

	Ebusiness Failures	Ebusiness Defenders	Ebusiness Cultivators	Ebusiness Successes
Characteristics	Termination due to improper financial management	Assumption of defensive posture due to adverse circumstances	Positive momentum and optimistic growth conditions	Trends of profitability, positive cashflow, and increased shareholder value
Examples	Boo.com, living.com	drkoop.com, CDNOW	Amazon.com	Yahoo!, eBay

The reality is that different firms can fall into different classifications at different times depending upon the particular organization's development and competitiveness. What naturally evolves from these labels is a continuum of ebusiness success upon which organizations are characterized. The continuum of ebusiness success is important to visualize when entering the online marketplace in that it guides managers toward organizational and financial success. A tendency among many contemporary managers is to measure success in terms of media recognition or positive investor sentiment. While these factors can certainly represent *signs* of success, they do not necessarily reflect long-term organizational prosperity.

Finding Success and Avoiding Failure: Digital Dimensioning

Regardless of an organization's circumstances—albeit start-up or fortified conglomerate—most aspire to the same general goals: to exploit present opportunities, strategically maneuver for new ones, and convert them all into results of high customer satisfaction, fortified financial strength, and increased company value. This aspiration is becoming an increasingly tall order, given the heightening environmental pressures of competition, legislation, and technology. At the same time, market behaviors of popularized start-ups have caused established organizations to question whether they should increase the pace of their strategic execution. Should advertising spending increase quickly because "high-flying" retailers are doing it? Should capital be raised since it seems like a behavior of many companies in our area? Should a major component of a work force be laid off to appease the investment community? These are all questions that flow through the minds of business leaders focusing on aspirations of commercial success.

The business environment's rapid evolution calls for new considerations on the part of entrepreneurs and management. It calls for a transformed business mentality that encompasses strategic thinking and conceptualization. It calls for a modified set of behaviors that avoids potential pitfalls and seizes market opportunities. Most importantly, it calls for a renewed discipline maximizing technological benefit in every organizational area without abandoning the fundamentals of commercial viability.

Digital Dimensioning is a professional's guide to achieving ebusiness success in every organization. This book presents a comprehensive model for helping organizations reach their objectives in spite of rapidly evolving technologies and aggressively moving competitors. The underlying model presented in *Digital Dimensioning* is designed to assist organizations of all sizes and stages of development to succeed. But since every organization's circumstances are somewhat unique, this book is not a definitive prescription for embracing ebusiness technology. The book is intended to be, instead, a practical resource for organizational members to evaluate their own particular ebusiness circumstances and move forward accordingly. Quite simply, *Digital Dimensioning* is a field guide to help managers perform an organizational self-diagnosis and subsequently build a unique prescription for digital success.

While many aspects of this book relate to technology, this book is not a technical guide. More accurately, it is a tool for managers striving to manage technical issues. Because of this, there are no descriptions of current technical tools, but there are guidelines for managing the influx of new technology as it becomes available to an organization and its competitors. At the same time, concepts in this book will not insist that managers execute strategies at a furious pace or develop business models that simply conform to current investor sentiment. Instead, this book will guide managers to proceed methodically according to the available resources of the organization as well as factors like the speed of online competitors and the realities of the marketplace. *Digital Dimensioning* will help managers build business models that focus on the profitable satisfaction of customers—an eventual "no-lose" situation for investors.

Perhaps most importantly, *Digital Dimensioning* will establish and reinforce the importance of companywide participation in ebusiness activities. In many organizations, digital activities such as Web site development are handled exclusively by marketing and information technology personnel. Understandably, the results of such activities are slanted toward the perspectives and interests of these organizational areas. In many cases, though, other areas of the organization are much more in tune with the resources of the organization and the needs of its customers. This book encourages organizations to analyze their functional activities and include personnel from each in the process of ebusiness development. Only through companywide involvement might an organization accurately recognize its challenges and adequately chart a course for meeting them.

Being in the midst of a business revolution like the one the Internet has created is captivating for managers and executives. Both the wild successes and dismal failures of Internet initiatives have presented a wealth of learning opportunities and new ideas. However, the realities of this new and tumultuous environment must be examined carefully as managers continue with existing initiatives and move forward with new ones. As you read this book, consider your organization and its path to ultimate ebusiness success against the backdrop of others that have succeeded or failed.

chapter 2

Digital Dimensioning: New-Era Management

Executive Preview

This chapter discusses the basics of digital dimensioning, the process of designing and implementing those digital activities that will best help an organization reach its goals. Digital dimensioning is presented as a series of steps:

(1) enlisting digital expertise,

(2) analyzing the digital environment,

(3) establishing digital direction,

(4) formulating digital strategy,

(5) implementing digital strategy, and

(6) controlling digital dimensioning.

Digital dimensioning is *not*, however, and should never be thought of as a manager's entire job. Instead, digital dimensioning is presented as a particular dimension of a manager's job that must appropriately complement the other major dimensions of the job. These other dimensions are planning, organizing, influencing, and controlling. The chapter opens with a discussion of Office Depot's formidable digital presence, and then provides digital dimensioning advice that a consultant could have given Office Depot management as input for initiating its digital presence. The chapter ends with resolutions that all managers can make to enhance the ebusiness competitiveness of *their* organizations.

Spotlight

Office Depot Recognized for Digital Excellence[1]

Office Depot, Inc., operates an international chain of more than 700 retail stores located in over 35 states, the District of Columbia, and five Canadian provinces. The stores carry a broad selection of merchandise including office supplies, business machines, computers, computer software, and office furniture. Each store has a multipurpose service center offering business-related services like printing and copying.

Office Depot recently gained significant national and international attention by appearing on Informationweek's ebusiness List of 100 Outstanding E-retailers in 1999. The Delray Beach, Florida, company initially designed its Web site, OfficeDepot.com, to cater to consumers and small businesses. At OfficeDepot.com customers place product orders and pay online, as well as check the status of their orders and inventories at Office Depot warehouses and stores around the country. Additionally, the site includes self-service functions like customers making lists of products they are most likely to buy and then placing repeat orders from those lists. The company benefits from OfficeDepot.com not only because the site generates new sales, but because the cost of filling Web-based orders is lower than the cost of filling traditional telephone orders.

By almost any measure, Office Depot's digital presence has been an outstanding success. According to Bill Seltzer, the vice president and chief information officer in charge of the site, plans for site improvement are already under way. Seltzer says that improvement will focus on continually bettering site functionality and speed.

Digital Dimensioning Principles

What's Ahead? The Spotlight mentioned several significant ways that Office Depot is focusing on gaining ebusiness competitiveness. Office Depot management is sending a clear message: To remain competitive in the future, the company must be ebusiness-competitive. The real challenge facing Office Depot management is taking the right steps to gain this competitiveness. This chapter focuses on these steps, which are applicable to virtually any organization, through a discussion of digital dimensioning.

Defining Digital Dimensioning

Defining *digital* and *dimensioning* individually yields a definition of the two terms collectively. As used in this book, the term *digital* refers to the Internet as well as other enhancing electronic technologies. This definition follows contemporary management vernacular more than traditional computer technology terminology. As implied by this definition, managers should consider electronic applications like wireless technology or voice recognition technology to enhance their Internet-based business applications.

Dimensioning is the process of crafting some object or entity with calculated intent. According to this definition, individuals design objects or entities to reflect specific concepts or ideas.

Combining the definitions of these two terms, *digital dimensioning* is the process of crafting some combination of Internet and supportive electronic technologies to solve business problems and resultantly help organizations reach their goals. In essence, the digital dimensioning process outlines the simple yet powerful steps that managers can take to gain ebusiness competitive advantage. Most fundamentally, the focus of this book is on employing the Internet in conjunction with other electronic technologies to solve business problems and thereby maximize organizational goal attainment.

In essence, digital dimensioning is a new, critical management function that modern managers must understand and practice to be successful in the new world of ebusiness. Digital dimensioning should always be aimed at achieving organizational goals. Managers shouldn't even attempt building digital thrust until they have a clear view of the organizational goals they are trying to achieve.

The Digital Dimensioning Process

Digital dimensioning is a process or series of steps. The major steps in this process, shown in Figure 2.1, are (1) enlisting digital expertise, (2) analyzing the digital environment, (3) establishing digital direction, (4) formulating digital strategy, (5) implementing digital strategy, and (6) controlling digital dimensioning. The following sections highlight each step and outline broad relationships among them. Future chapters discuss each step in detail. The chapters corresponding to each step are shown in Figure 2.1.

Figure 2.1   Steps of the digital dimensioning process and the chapters that explain them.

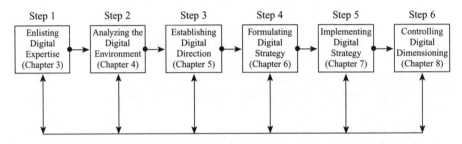

Step 1: Enlisting Digital Expertise   Like any organizational effort, digital dimensioning activities will be successful *only if* individuals with appropriate skills perform them. These skills involve technical skill, people skill, and conceptual skill. *Technical skill* is the ability to use ebusiness technology resources appropriately, while *people skill* is the ability to influence stakeholders to become focused and involved in carrying out ebusiness activities. The third skill, *conceptual skill*, is the ability to see the organization as a whole and design ebusiness activities to suit that view.

If managers do not have sufficient digital expertise in their organizations, many options are available to enlist it. First, management can train present organization members so that they develop needed digital expertise. Such training must be based upon carefully designed programs aimed at enhancing digital expertise deficiencies. Interestingly, IBM recently found that training people internally just wasn't a quick enough alternative to providing needed digital expertise. To accelerate its process of attaining the digital expertise it needed, IBM bought Aragon Consulting Group of St. Louis, an ebusiness marketing strategy and research company. This IBM acquisition typifies several of IBM's other acquisitions aimed at quickly gaining Internet expertise to meet overwhelming internal and client demand for ebusiness services.

A second option to enlist needed digital expertise in an organization is to hire new organization members who already possess the expertise. A carefully focused recruitment effort can yield significant increases in digital expertise within an organization in a relatively short time. Recruiting employees with valuable digital expertise, however, may not be an easy task. As more companies look to integrate both Internet and intranet applications into their business models, digital expertise has become a core competency that virtually all organizations are attempting to develop. Naturally, this increased demand for people with ebusiness expertise has made it more difficult to find such potential employees and has heightened salary costs related to hiring them. This high demand also makes it difficult for an organization in today's economy to retain their ebusiness professionals once hired.

A third option to enlist needed digital expertise in an organization is to engage the assistance of outside consultants. Hiring such a firm can immediately supply a manager with a wealth of needed digital expertise. Management must keep in mind, however, that hiring such a contractor is not an automatic solution for ebusiness problems. Instead, a contractor will generally help to solve management's ebusiness problems only if the contractor possesses the needed people, technical, and conceptual skills that are prerequisites for ebusiness success. Hiring outside consultants without these skills can be disastrous, resulting in having a consulting partner too preoccupied with incidentals like speed to market, too prone to cost overruns, and reluctant to ask for needed expertise that exists only outside the consulting firms. Management will find an appropriate consulting firm only by exercising appropriate due diligence.

This section introduces the notion that enlisting digital expertise in an organization is a prerequisite for gaining ebusiness success. Managers must conscientiously monitor the level of digital expertise in organizations and maintain that level necessary to carry out desired digital thrust. Without involving digital expertise appropriately, the ebusiness activities of any organization are destined for failure. Chapter 3, "Enlisting Digital Expertise," discusses in detail how to provide digital skill for organizations.

Step 2: Analyzing the Digital Environment   After enlisting appropriate digital expertise, the next step of the digital dimensioning process is analyzing an organization's digital environment. This analysis includes monitoring, assessing, and making conclusions about organizational surroundings that could impact the organization's ebusiness activities. The purpose of the analysis is to clearly define factors that can impact an organization's digital presence both today and in the future. The analysis focuses on all critical factors both inside and outside the organization that could influence progress toward building ebusiness competitive advantage. From organization to organization, these factors may be varied, but usually include issues like the types and nature of suppliers, pending legislation, and the ebusiness activities of competitors.

For an example illustrating the importance of management understanding an organization's digital environment, consider recent developments in the digital environment of major utility companies. Industry experts are voicing with more regularity the opinion that although relatively few utility companies are presently allowing residential customers to pay bills online, many such companies will likely offer the option in the near future. These experts are also expressing the opinion that the Internet is an invaluable medium that utility companies can use to gain significant competitive advantage.

One notable utility company reacting to this evolution of the digital environment was Consumers Energy, the principal subsidiary of CMS Energy Corporation.[2] Consumers Energy management considered this expert opinion along with its personal knowledge that many of its customers owned computers, many were currently online, and many would like the convenience of paying bills online. Further, Consumers Energy management knew of the growing popularity of the Internet within society as a whole, and of advances in encryption technology that seemed to make online bill paying technically viable. Management also knew that cutting operational expenses by having customers key in their own billing information seemed to make online bill paying financially beneficial.

Considering all of this digital environment information, Consumers Energy management initiated a new online service that allowed residential customers to review and pay their natural gas or electric bill through the utility's Web site. Five weeks after the initiation of the program, almost 6500 out of 2.4 million customers had begun to pay their bills online. The company expects a significant proportion of its customers to be paying bills online within 2 years. The company seems to be well on its way to establishing competitive advantage through digital applications.

Overall, to be successful in establishing ebusiness competitive advantage, a manager must make the digital activities of an organization consistent with its digital environment. Chapter 4, "Analyzing the Digital Environment," discusses how to build this consistency.

Step 3: Establishing Digital Direction   In the third step of the digital dimensioning process, managers establish the digital direction that their organizations will take. Step 3 builds on the results of steps 1 and 2. That is, a manager builds the direction of an organization's digital activities only after he or she has enlisted appropriate digital expertise and thoroughly understands the organization's digital environment. This step entails making digital direction tangible through a mission statement and related goals. Naturally, the digitally oriented mission statement and goals can be independent organizational exhibits or be presented as components of the organization's overall mission statement and goals. Chapter 5 discusses the statement of digital direction and digital support goals as components to establish digital direction.

One critical factor influencing digital direction in an organization is management's overall philosophy about pursuing digital activities. Consider the reported philosophy of management toward pursuing digital activities at Ryerson Tull, Inc.[3] The company, headquartered in Chicago, is North America's largest distributor and processor of metals and industrial plastics, and has annual sales of approximately $3 billion. In addition, Ryerson Tull has more than 70 facilities in North America, has joint-venture relationships in Mexico, India, and China, and has over 5000 employees worldwide.

At Ryerson Tull, management's philosophy toward digital activities is that a company should not wait to create, in some think tank environment, the best digital strategy that will solve all its industry problems at once. Instead, a company should engage in real digital activities and learn from experience about how to solve industry problems. Implied in this philosophy is the idea that companies should learn about digital activities through trial and error, and probably start with small digital projects and eventually graduate to larger and larger projects. Following this philosophy, Ryerson Tull is pursuing basic digital activities aimed at offering customers digital solutions to an array of fundamental business problems. Additionally, the company has become an equity partner in an industry-related portal. Given management's philosophy about how to pursue digital activities, expect Ryerson Tull to modify, heighten, or even change its array of digital activities based upon what it has learned over time from its involvement in the digital arena.

As you might suspect, determining the appropriate digital direction for an organization is extremely important. Chapter 5, "Establishing Digital Direction," discusses how to establish such direction and introduces the digital support grid, a new management tool designed to help improve the accomplishment of digital goals.

Step 4: Formulating Digital Strategy   The fourth step of the digital dimensioning process, formulating digital strategy, focuses on achieving the organization's digital goals. Overall, this step involves building a plan that outlines how the organization will reach its ebusiness goals as outlined in step 3. Once a manager has analyzed the digital environment of an organization and has set digital direction, he or she is ready to build a strategy for reaching digital goals. Chapter 6, "Formulating Digital Strategy," discusses in detail how to develop this strategy.

Recent events at Dow Chemical Company clearly show how goals can give rise to digital strategy. Dow Chemical Company is a global organization that develops and manufactures scientific and technology-based products, such as those used in chemicals, plastics, and agriculture. The company has customers all around the world, with operations in North America, Europe, Latin America, the Pacific, and Africa.

One goal established at Dow is to make the company a sustainable growth company. To focus on achieving this goal, Dow adopted the digital strategy of investing very heavily in ebusiness activities. Dow is investing millions of dollars to transform its century-old manufacturing business into a world-renowned business with a significant ebusiness base. Dow still makes the same products, but through ebusiness activities it is becoming a more precise, lower-cost supplier. The company plans to leverage the Internet to sell high-margin engineering and other services that complement its core businesses. To bring focus and accountability to this new digital thrust, the company has even established a new position, Vice President of e-Business.[4]

Step 5: Implementing Digital Strategy   This fifth step of the digital dimensioning process is implementing digital strategy. Since, at this stage, the manager has now completed steps 1 through 4 of the digital dimensioning process, he or she is now ready to intelligently put that digital strategy into action. The manager has enlisted digital expertise, analyzed the organization's digital environment, established a direction for digital focus, formulated a strategy for achieving the established direction, and is now ready to implement the strategy.

In order to implement digital strategy successfully, managers must perform activities such as allocating the resources necessary to build the systems required and engaging in adequate planning. Also, knowing how to change an organization to enhance digital focus is typically very valuable to a manager during digital strategy implementation. Chapter 7, "Implementing Digital Strategy," gives managers detailed advice on how to put digital strategy into action.

Consider events at DaimlerChrysler as an illustration of how digital strategy formulation relates to digital strategy implementation.[5] DaimlerChrysler manufactures a wide array of products, including passenger cars, trucks, and commercial and military aircraft. Perhaps the company's most well-known passenger cars are Mercedes-Benz and Chrysler. DaimlerChrysler recently adopted the digital strategy of significantly upgrading its ebusiness infrastructure in order to remain competitive. To achieve this upgrading, the company conceptualized FastCar, a project aimed at delivering built-to-order cars on a mass scale. FastCar is planned to provide Internet communication links among company suppliers, designers, engineers, and purchasing agents.

Now that the FastCar strategy has been formulated, the next challenge for management at DaimlerChrysler is implementing the strategy. To accomplish this, it is critical to develop the digital infrastructure needed to support FastCar, establish needed relationships with suppliers involved in FastCar, and train people in using FastCar. Regardless of management's perceived value of FastCar as a digital strategy, FastCar will be of no worth to DaimlerChrysler if it cannot be implemented successfully.

Step 6: Controlling Digital Dimensioning   Controlling an organization's digital dimensioning activities is a special type of organizational control. This control focuses on monitoring and evaluating the digital dimensioning process to make sure that the results of digital dimensioning activities materialize as planned. Essentially, controlling digital dimensioning entails monitoring digital activities to ensure that digital goals are achieved. While controlling digital dimensioning, if digital goals aren't achieved, management might be required to take action, such as improving digital strategy, improving the way digital strategy is implemented, or reviewing the results of the analysis of the digital environment to see if digital goals were set too high. Management must keep in mind that controlling digital dimensioning might even include improving the process used to control digital dimensioning. Chapter 8, "Controlling Digital Dimensioning," explains in detail what managers should do to make sure that digital dimensioning activities are properly controlled.

When controlling digital dimensioning activities, managers must be aware that action taken to improve the effectiveness of digital activities, once implemented, should be monitored very carefully. In some cases, improvements aimed at enhancing the attainment of digital goals will indeed be effective and will result in the goals being achieved. In other cases, however, such improvements may create new issues that actually increase the difficulty of reaching digital goals.

Recent events at Luminate Software Corporation illustrate that activities aimed at making digital improvements can actually result in issues that management must handle before digital success can be achieved.[6] Luminate provides organizations with comprehensive Internet infrastructure for ebusiness applications. Through a product called Luminate.Net, the company offers its customers an outsourcing service that frees customers from certain significant ebusiness costs in areas related to hardware, software, and installation. Essentially, Luminate positions itself as the means that customer IT departments can use to keep up with the continuing whirlwind developments in ebusiness applications and related technology.

Luminate recently launched a new Web site showcasing a new, improvement-oriented digital service. With this new service, the company could deliver its software to customers over the Internet rather than follow its old practice of physically installing it on-site. The new service came about as a result of management's observation that the practice of on-site software installation was losing momentum in the marketplace while the practice of providing software via the Internet was gaining momentum.

Negative reaction to Luminate's announced improvement-oriented change was swift and significant. The day after the new Internet service was launched, the company received hundreds of mostly complaining emails. Interestingly, the emails came primarily from people inside Luminate rather than from customers. Some believe that employees reacted in this fashion because management, for the most part, announced the Internet-based software delivery change to employees at the same time it presented it to the customers and did not involve employees in formulating the improvement-oriented plans.

The lesson seems clear. Regardless of the validity of planned digital improvements, the success of those improvements can be negatively influenced by the implementation. At Luminate, management's implementation of the improvements seemed to precipitate significant negative employee reaction. Only by neutralizing such negative reaction can Luminate management create an environment in which the improvements can bring maximum benefit to the organization.

Overall, the digital dimensioning process can be viewed as a series of discrete steps, or as illustrated in Figure 2.2, as many steps applied as a whole. Certainly, this "discrete-steps" approach facilitates learning

Figure 2.2 Managers may sometimes consider all digital dimensioning steps together.

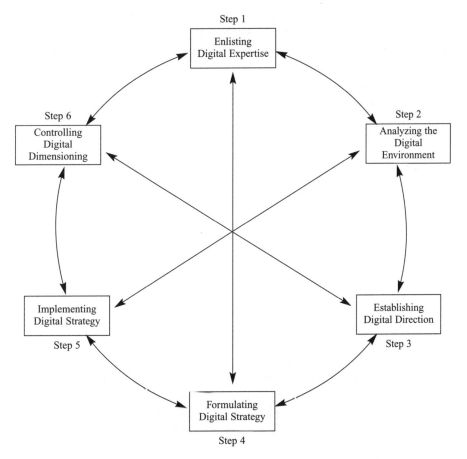

Step 1
Enlisting
Digital Expertise

Step 6
Controlling
Digital
Dimensioning

Step 2
Analyzing the
Digital
Environment

Implementing
Digital Strategy
Step 5

Establishing
Digital Direction
Step 3

Formulating
Digital Strategy
Step 4

about digital dimensioning. In practice, however, managers may sometimes find that digital dimensioning requires working on two or more steps at the same time, or even working on the steps in a somewhat different order. In reality, managers must not focus on any one step of the digital dimensioning process without considering one or more other steps. For example, managers should not formulate digital strategy without considering how it might be implemented and controlled. Figure 2.2 illustrates that with digital dimensioning, managers may sometimes find themselves considering several or even all digital dimensioning steps together.

Digital Dimensioning and Strategic Management

Strategic management is long-range planning that focuses on moving the organization as a whole toward achieving organizational goals.[7] In managing strategically, managers consider the organization as a total unit and ask themselves what must be done in the long term to reach established targets. Long term is usually defined as a period of time extending about 3 to 5 years into the future. Thus, in essence, when managing strategically, managers are trying to determine what to do now to be successful in 3 to 5 years. Traditionally performed major tasks of strategic management include analyzing organizational environment, establishing organizational direction, formulating organizational strategy, and implementing and controlling organizational strategy.

Upon reflection, the digital dimensioning process seems somewhat similar to the strategic management process. The similarity between strategic management goals like "analyzing the organizational environment" and digital dimensioning goals like "analyzing the digital environment" points up the similarity. Overall, it is helpful to think of digital dimensioning and strategic management as somewhat similar processes, but with digital dimensioning having much narrower scope and purpose. Strategic management aims at developing a logic concerning all organizational functions, whereas digital dimensioning aims at developing a logic concerning digital functions.

Management must establish the unique relationship between strategic management and digital dimensioning as determined by distinctive organizational needs. In some organizations with established strategic management processes, perhaps the digital dimensioning process can be thought of primarily as a subset of the strategic management process. In such cases, simply by establishing the digital dimensioning process as a special subset of the strategic management process, management can ensure that digital dimensioning receives the necessary attention.

In organizations that do not have an established strategic management process, perhaps the digital dimensioning process should be established as a special, unique organizational process, thus making sure that the digital thrust receives the attention it needs. In such organizations, digital dimensioning should not be thought of as a substitute for strategic management. Instead, it should be considered a process that gives strategic focus to an important organizational ingredient, online presence.

Management must be careful to avoid the opinion that issues in the digital environment change so rapidly that digital dimensioning is relatively valueless. Stories abound of organizations going from an idea to a business plan to a tangible online company in a matter of only months. Many such companies, once established, reportedly maintain a hectic pace of quickly reacting to changes in environmental factors like competitive positioning or technology advances. Management of such companies seems to be constantly uncovering digital environment issues and responding to them quickly and often.

Granted, digital times may require that managers respond to the digital environment changes in such a manner. Such quick and frequent changes, however, do not reduce the need for sound digital dimensioning, but, rather, increase it. Management should strenuously avoid the dangerous pitfall of forgoing thoughtful digital dimensioning because the process seemingly takes too long or requires too much energy. Without thoughtful digital dimensioning, success becomes simply a matter of almost random chance rather than of management expertise.

Digital Dimensioning: The Manager's Whole Job?

This book presents digital dimensioning as a major activity that modern managers must perform to gain ebusiness competitiveness in the new, digital era of business. Digital dimensioning, however, is not and should never be seen as a manager's entire job. Management is the process of working with and through people and other organizational resources to accomplish organizational goals.[8] Wisdom accumulated over the last century by practicing managers as well as management scholars indicates that managers manage by performing four primary activities: planning, organizing, influencing, and controlling.

Given the burgeoning growth of the new digital business environment, however, it seems critical that managers include digital dimensioning as a primary management activity along with planning, organizing, influencing, and controlling. In essence, digital dimensioning should impact the way a manager plans, organizes, influences, and controls. Conversely, planning, organizing, influencing, and controlling should influence the way managers are using the process of digital dimensioning. Figure 2.3 illustrates this general relationship between digital dimensioning and the more historically accepted management functions. The following sections discuss these historical functions and their relationship with digital dimensioning more fully.

Figure 2.3 Digital dimensioning has an impact on and is impacted by traditional management functions.

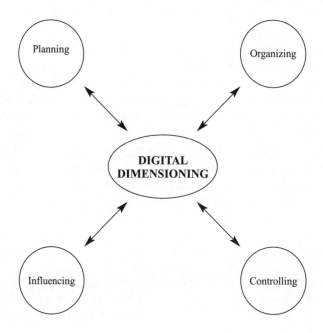

Planning

Planning is the process of establishing organizational goals, choosing tasks that must be performed in order to reach those goals, outlining how the tasks should be performed, and determining when the tasks should be performed. Absolutely, planning focuses on goal accomplishment. Through plans, managers outline what must be done to reach goals.

Planning is indeed valuable to managers for many different reasons. First, planning activities help managers to focus on the future. In order to plan, managers must concentrate on future problems rather than everyday problems. Such a focus on the future helps managers to identify and solve problems on the horizon. Planning is also valuable to managers because it emphasizes a culture that requires management decisions to be made only after considering the impact of the decisions on today's operations as well as future events. Decisions made in the present without reflecting on the future can cause unwanted dysfunctionality in organizations. Lastly, planning is valuable to managers because it constantly focuses on organizational goals. Keeping organizational goals in the forefront of management minds helps management constantly strive to reach those goals. As a result, planning helps managers focus on success, the attainment of organizational goals.

According to Figure 2.3, planning can impact digital dimensioning and digital dimensioning can impact planning. Planning can impact digital dimensioning, for example, if a manager applies planning knowledge to structure goals for the organization's digital dimensioning thrust. On the other hand, digital dimensioning can impact planning if a manager designs and establishes an intranet component that allows employees throughout the world to have efficient and valuable input on what organizational plans should be.

Organizing

Organizing is the process of establishing orderly uses for all resources within an organization. Resources include the organization's people, raw materials, equipment, and financial assets. In determining orderly uses, managers focus on how to use resources to best carry out plans aimed at reaching organizational goals. Organizing assists managers in making objectives apparent throughout the organization and emphasizing to specific individuals or groups the tasks outlined during planning. In essence, organizing assigns work that, once completed, will result in the organization reaching its targets. Organizing schemes are built on the notion that the output of individuals results in success for departments, which in turn results in success for divisions, which in turn results in success for the entire organization.

Organizing is extremely important to management because organizing is the vehicle for turning plans into action. The organizing process establishes relationships among all organizational resources by indicating which resources are to be used for what tasks, when they are to be used, where they are to be used, and how they are to be used. Major organizing efforts in organizations include coordinating activities, defining jobs people perform, establishing supervisory relationships, and assigning equipment.

Certainly, organizing can impact digital dimensioning. For example, managers organize when establishing who should do what jobs in the digital dimensioning effort. The people assigned to carry out digital dimensioning activities will certainly have impact on the success of digital thrust. The quality of equipment purchased, also an organizing issue, will certainly impact the success of digital efforts. While poor-quality equipment can render digital efforts unreliable and of little value, high-quality equipment can enhance the overall perception and success of digital efforts.

Digital dimensioning can also impact organizing. For example, it directly affects how a manager coordinates activities among different divisions throughout the world via Internet videoconferencing. Caterpillar is an example of a company that has been a strong proponent of such videoconferencing for more than a decade.[9] Caterpillar manufactures products such as construction and mining equipment, diesel and natural gas engines, and industrial gas turbines. Although Caterpillar is headquartered in Peoria, Illinois, the company has significant operations in Indonesia, Italy, Japan, Mexico, Northern Ireland, and Poland. In this company, videoconferencing plays an important role in coordinating projects that span Caterpillar's global facilities. With continuing advances in technological development that make video-conferencing more effective, efficient, and Internet-compatible, such communication at companies like Caterpillar will inevitably become more common in the future.

Influencing

Influencing is the process of guiding the activities of people in appropriate directions. Appropriate directions, of course, are those that lead to the attainment of organizational goals. Influencing involves focusing on employees as people and dealing with such issues as morale, arbitration of conflict, and the development of positive working relationships. For many managers, success is primarily determined by how well they influence others.

The process of influencing people in organizations entails four primary activities: leading, motivating, managing groups, and communicating. Certainly, these four steps are related. To illustrate this interrelationship, managers should decide what kind of leadership style they should employ only after they determine what kind of group they are leading and how that group can best be motivated. In addition, communication between managers is the primary means of employing leadership style, motivating others, and working with groups. The influencing process emphasizes that motivating, communicating, managing groups, and leading are all aimed at encouraging appropriate behavior and thus reaching organizational goals.

Managers must keep in mind that how they influence others can impact the success of digital dimensioning efforts. For example, how a manager attempts to motivate individuals performing digital dimensioning activities can affect the quality of work those individuals produce. If the manager attempts to motivate mainly through punitive means, workers may produce high-quality digital dimensioning output in the short run. In the long run, however, such a motivation plan will probably result in a diminishing quality of output. Naturally, this diminishing quality of work will lessen the success of digital efforts.

Digital dimensioning can also impact the success of management's influencing efforts. For example, as a means of motivating organization members, many managers choose to award gift certificates to people who do outstanding work. For some companies, it might make sense to award gift certificates and have employees redeem those gift certificates on the organization's intranet or Web site. For other organizations, it might make sense to enlist the services of an organization specializing in the design and administration of such programs. Some programs, like those at GiftCertificates.com, are Internet-based.[10]

GiftCertificates.com offers a special gift certificate, called the SuperCertificate, which stresses maximum flexibility. Recipients can use their SuperCertificates to personally choose their gifts, or redeem SuperCertificates for gift certificates at over 500 popular stores, restaurants, travel merchants, Internet retailers, spas, and movie theaters. SuperCertificates can be exchanged for gift certificates from well-known retailers like J.Crew, Macy's, Barnes & Noble, Sam Goody, and Bloomingdale's. Conceptually, such flexible rewards for doing good work motivate employees to continue doing good work.

Controlling

Controlling is the process of making sure that events occur as planned. As implied by this definition, planning and controlling should be thought of as inseparable, the Siamese twins of management. Planning is a manager's map showing how to reach organizational goals. Certainly, without such a map, consistently achieving organizational targets would be highly unlikely. Simply having a plan, however, doesn't guarantee success in attaining organizational goals. The plan needs to be reviewed periodically to ensure that all the right steps are being taken. Sometimes, a planning review leads to the conclusion that the plan should be changed, perhaps because circumstances have changed or because the plan was improperly conceived.

Murphy's law states that anything that can go wrong will go wrong. Murphy's law, however, is not a harbinger of inevitable difficulty in performing organizational activities. Rather, managers should think of controlling as the means for avoiding the inevitably of Murphy's law. From a management viewpoint, Murphy's law takes effect largely due to poor controlling. In the world of management, anything that can go wrong will go wrong only if it isn't controlled properly. Management should continually gather information about progress being made in the organization, comparing that progress with expected or planned progress, and based upon this comparison, making any necessary changes to ensure that actual progress reaches planned levels.

Controlling can certainly impact the success of digital dimensioning. For example, assume that an organization's digital plan has been designed and implemented, but management lacks a focus on controlling digital efforts. Here, management believes that controlling is important, but has been only haphazardly monitoring digital efforts to gauge digital progress. Such a monitoring pattern will not afford management the best opportunity to uncover and neutralize issues slowing the progress of digital activities. As a result, management maximization of digital efforts based upon controlling will be virtually nonexistent.

In addition to controlling being able to impact digital dimensioning, digital dimensioning can certainly impact controlling. Consider recently reported events at T.G.I. Friday's as an illustration.[11] T.G.I. Friday's is a chain of full-service, casual dining restaurants featuring a wide selection of freshly prepared, popular foods and beverages served in a relaxed setting. Friday's digital system was purposefully designed to include features for providing management with a continuing stream of evaluative digital information, including the number of people visiting the company Web site, times of the day and days of the week when the Web site was most visited, and the length of time each visitor stayed after entering the Web site. In essence, digital activities at Friday's were designed to include the generation of information that could help management to control digital efforts, improving the company's Web site.

Upon reviewing such information about the company's Web site, Friday's management recently came to the conclusion that the site needed to be improved. Consistent with the visitors' experience that management tries to create for restaurant visitors, management aimed site improvements at helping site visitors to have an enjoyable time during their visit. As a result, the site was modified to be very entertaining and engaging. Perhaps the most enjoyable feature of the revised site is the "Mixology" section that links several mixed specialty drinks served at Fridays to their recipes. Naturally, the site informs visitors that they must be over 21 years old to use the site.

Friday's was among the first restaurants to launch a Web site. Instead of being satisfied with its initial Web site effort, however, management is using digital information to help control and improve it. Over time, site improvement of this sort should continue to build not only the number of visitors to the Friday's Web site, but also the number of visitors to Friday's restaurants.

Back to Office Depot

The purpose of this section is to illustrate how digital dimensioning principles apply to real organizations. Consider the following information as digital dimensioning advice that an ebusiness consultant might have given Office Depot management as input for initiating its digital presence. To gain maximum benefit from this section, explore OfficeDepot.com before reading further.

"As management at Office Depot you must understand that for your company to remain successful in the long run, it must be ebusiness-competitive. Certainly, your competitors like Staples and Corporate Express are making plans and taking steps to make great strides in digital retailing. To keep up with competitors, you must focus on digital dimensioning, continually choosing and putting into action those digital activities that will best help Office Depot reach its goals.

"In digital dimensioning at Office Depot, take the following steps:

- **_Enlist digital expertise at Office Depot._** You must evaluate very carefully the employees at Office Depot based upon the amount of digital expertise they possess. From the results of this evaluation, determine if adequate digital expertise at Office Depot exists. If improvement is necessary, consider some combination of

  (1) hiring new employees with needed digital expertise,

  (2) training present employees in deficient digital skill areas, and

  (3) engaging a professional ebusiness consultant.

- **_Analyze Office Depot's digital environment._** You must define in detail Office Depot's digital surroundings. This analysis should answer diverse questions like

  (1) What kind of ebusiness activities are competitors like Office Max presently performing?

  (2) What digital services do Office Depot customers need?

  (3) How does Office Depot's marketing work?

  (4) Is Office Depot successful in recruiting talented employees?

- **_Establish Office Depot's digital direction._** Establish Office Depot's digital direction once you enlist appropriate digital expertise and understand the company's digital environment. Establishing digital direction involves establishing Office Depot's mission and goals for its digital initiatives. For example, you may discover during environmental analysis that there is usually a shortage of talented employees in most Office Depot stores. As a result, you could establish a digital direction goal of assisting individual Office Depot stores throughout the world in recruiting talented employees.

- **_Formulate Office Depot's digital strategy._** After establishing company digital goals for Office Depot, you should develop the company's digital strategy. This step involves outlining the plan for achieving digital goals. Continuing with the above sample goal, you might establish the plan of designing a 'Find a Job' section for the corporate Web site that enables visitors to explore positions available in each Office Depot store. Part of the plan might include email capability, allowing visitors to the corporate site who are interested in certain job openings to email directly the managers of those stores where the openings exist.

- *Implement Office Depot's digital strategy.* Implementing Office Depot's digital strategy is putting its plan for reaching digital goals into action. For the above 'Find a Job' example, in this step you would face actually constructing and putting into action the new portion of the site aimed at recruiting. You would ensure actions like setting up systems to receive notification of openings from Office Depot stores throughout the world, loading the openings on the corporate site, and establishing the process for taking job openings off the site when the positions are filled.

- *Control Office Depot's digital dimensioning.* By controlling Office Depot's digital dimensioning, you make sure that the digital activities are having proper impact. Again continuing on with 'Find a Job,' you might ensure an action like monitoring the new site feature to see if it is working technically. Controlling here could also involve checking to see if the new 'Find a Job' section has actually been successful in recruiting new, needed talent. If the site is not working technically, make sure it is debugged. If needed employees are not being recruited via the site as planned, explore changes like modifying the 'Find a Job' content or enhancing the site's visual design. In other words, take steps to find out why 'Find a Job' isn't getting expected results and make sure that the necessary changes are made.

"When you perform the above digital dimensioning steps to bring digital success to Office Depot, it may sometimes seem that you should perform them sequentially in discrete steps. In reality, to ensure the success of your digital dimensioning efforts, no step should be performed without giving consideration to the other steps. For example, you should not implement the 'Find a Job' strategy without thinking about how it can be controlled and the digital direction that it reflects.

"Remember that in order for you to succeed at Office Depot, digital dimensioning is only one part of a manager's complete job, the others being planning, organizing, influencing, and controlling. Use what you know about planning, organizing, influencing, and controlling to enhance the success of digital dimensioning. Conversely, use what you know about digital dimensioning to help carry out planning, organizing, influencing, and controlling."

Digital Dimensioning Resolutions

- Take every opportunity to convince organization members that ebusiness is critical for ensuring the success of modern organizations.

- Use the definition of digital dimensioning as the rationale for stressing that digital efforts must be linked closely to achieving established organizational goals.

- Include people with digital skills in your digital dimensioning.

- Thoroughly analyze your digital environment to make sure that your ebusiness foundation is solid.

- Clarify and promote your philosophy about ebusiness as a driving force in your organization.

- Establish a clear mission with related goals for your ebusiness activities.

- Establish clear steps for achieving your ebusiness goals.

- Put your steps for achieving ebusiness goals into action.

- Monitor your steps for achieving ebusiness goals and make improvements when necessary.

- Combine digital dimensioning efforts with planning, organizing, influencing, and controlling efforts to maximize the attainment of organizational goals.

chapter 3

Enlisting Digital Expertise

Executive Preview

This chapter explores the nature of selecting and organizing the appropriate personnel for carrying out various digital dimensioning activities. It describes the different types and degrees of digital expertise. The chapter goes on to explain the differing skill requirements of various digital dimensioning activities and then takes up the task of surveying the organization for the presence and availability of required skills. Next, the focus shifts to the process of looking outside the organization for expertise when it is not fully present inside the organization. Once the appropriate expertise is identified, there are a variety of options for assembling those selected. The chapter also explains the intricacies of involving a cross-functional group of personnel to ensure that digital activities address objectives across the entire organization. The chapter begins with fundamentals presented in the practical context of Fiserv, a global leader in software and services for the financial services sector that exercises prudent practices in assembling digital personnel. This thread is picked up in the latter part of the chapter, with recommendations that an ebusiness consultant might have given Fiserv with respect to chapter concepts. The chapter ends with selected resolutions that readers can make to effectively include and manage human resources with respect to digital activities.

Fiserv Mines Internal and External Resources for Digital Expertise

Fiserv, Inc., provides enterprise software and services to financial institutions around the world. With over 13,000 employees and 10,000 institutional customers worldwide, the ebusiness opportunities for Fiserv are more than considerable. One of Fiserv's wholly owned business units is CBS Worldwide, an operating entity that installs and services enterprise software for international banking clients. While new-economy pressures are certainly felt by Fiserv, CBS Worldwide, its calculated approach to involving skilled personnel has enabled it to convert digital challenges into opportunities.

For each new ebusiness initiative, the management of Fiserv, CBS Worldwide, forms a dedicated team according to the project's skill requirements and business objectives. Each team is led by a project champion and executive sponsor who coordinate selected personnel. The teams typically include personnel from marketing, sales, product management, finance, and human resources in some cases. The cross-functional orientation of Fiserv's teams brings broad organizational perspective to projects. According to senior management, an absence of cross-functionality usually leads to deliverables that fail to address the broader objectives of the organization. When internal personnel are not available to meet a project's requirements, Fiserv looks outside the organization to enlist outside contractors and vendors that can bring required skills to the table.

Fiserv has developed a reputation for delivering on-time, on-budget enterprise software implementations. Its ability to do so has been based in part on a sound approach to bringing appropriate skills to bear. What's more, Fiserv's management actively seeks and enlists expertise with inherent characteristics necessary to thriving in the age of digital technology.

Fundamentals of Enlisting Digital Expertise

What's Ahead? The Spotlight described Fiserv's approach to identifying and organizing the expertise necessary to successfully perform digital activities. After determining the nature and scope of the digital tasks at hand, Fiserv senior management first takes steps to identify the skills necessary to complete the tasks successfully. Once such skills are identified, management then evaluates its personnel to determine whether all of the skills are within the organization or not. To acquire those skill sets that are not present or readily available, management looks outside the organization for supplementary competencies. Fiserv's approach seems relatively simple in theory. Taking such steps to make informed decisions about digital expertise, however, involves a calculated decision-making methodology. This chapter suggests such an approach in full detail to give managers a road map for understanding digital expertise, identifying internal and external sources of the expertise, and managing the collective expertise once assembled.

Enlisting Digital Expertise: A Focus on Process

Chapter 1 explained the need for digital dimensioning, making the point that organizations risk dire financial consequences, even failure, if management does not embrace a calculated approach to growth and evolution. Digital dimensioning becomes the difference between success and failure within the context of business in the new economy. The first step of the digital dimensioning process—enlisting digital expertise—is the primary focus of this chapter.

Arguably, the most precious resource of an organization is the expertise of its personnel. Many use the term *human capital* to refer to employees, a term that implies the high value added to the organization through the presence of talented employees. Even the most established infrastructure, distinguishable competitive advantages, and synergistic business partnerships are almost worthless without skilled personnel to execute and perform on a daily basis. The speed and fervor of the new economy makes personnel issues very challenging. Periods of low unemployment make the notion of retention critical because the challenge of replacing workers is considerable if they are lost. For this reason, progressive organizations take a variety of steps to recruit and retain personnel. To do this, many companies use incentives, benefits, and a positive organizational culture. Southwest Airlines, known for its friendly and nurturing workplace culture, has been named among the top companies to work for in America based upon its attentiveness to employees, sometimes even over its customers. All these managerial tactics are intended to attract and retain workers in an effort to profitably meet the needs of customers.

Like just about every other business function, successfully completing digital activities requires personnel with appropriate skills. Managers must be fully aware of all considerations surrounding the selection and assembly of those involved. A focus on personnel and skill issues begins with an examination of the rigorous process whereby the skill requirements of digital activities are met by the selection and assembly of qualified personnel. Enlisting expertise, as the first step of the digital dimensioning process, is a process in itself. Figure 3.1 is a graphical depiction of this process. Keep in mind that this process is intended to serve as a road map for managers seeking to meet the human resource needs of digital activities. As you read this chapter, it may be helpful to refer to Figure 3.1 often to fully absorb the flow and logic of the process.

The process itself is composed of a series of progressive steps. As you can see in Figure 3.1, the first step (box 1) is to recognize and understand the three different types of skill—technical, people, and conceptual—involved in digital activities. Managers must understand not only the distinctions between such skills but the notion that each skill can be obtained in varying degrees. Having *some* skill in a given area does not necessarily ensure that a person has *enough* of that skill to complete certain tasks. Box 2 of Figure 3.1 represents the next step of enlisting digital expertise. Quite simply, this step calls on managers to understand that different digital activities require various degrees of those skills described in box 1. Only through a grasp of a digital activity's skill requirements can a manager understand which sources of digital expertise are essential. Once the manager identifies the personnel skills and digital activity skills needed, the manager must then undertake the task of surveying the organization for the presence and availability of those skills. This step is graphically represented in box 3. When a manager examines an organization to locate the qualified expertise required to complete digital activities, there are three possible results he or she will likely find. The first possibility (box 3a) is that *all* required skills are pres-

Figure 3.1   The managerial process for enlisting the person-
             nel necessary to successfully complete digital
             dimensioning activities.

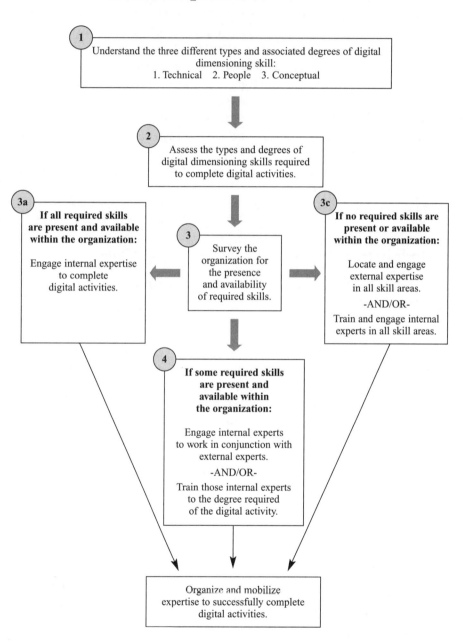

ent and available within the organization. In this case, managers can engage internal personnel to participate in the digital dimensioning process. A second possibility (box 3b) is that only *some* required skills are present and available within the organization. This result calls for management to engage both internal and external personnel to success- fully complete the digital activities. Still a third possibility (box 3c) is that no required skills are available within the organization to support digital dimensioning efforts. When managers see this result, they must rely com- pletely on external sources to meet the requirements of digital activities. Regardless of the outcome of the manager's exploration for skills within the organization, the next challenge for the manager is to organize and mobilize the identified sources of expertise in an effort to carry out the digital dimensioning process. This step is depicted in box 4 of Figure 3.1. This chapter will explore each step of this process in depth to pro- vide insight into the very crucial considerations of personnel.

Understanding Digital Dimensioning Skills

As indicated in Figure 3.1, the first step in enlisting expertise is under- standing the expertise itself. When evaluating the digital skills of current or potential personnel, there are many difficulties. First of all, there is very little precedent for defining an employee's knowledge base in the context of ebusiness and ecommerce. Unlike in the more established areas of professional service such as law, finance, or operations man- agement, there is no formal certification or licensing of management in the new economy. And there is also a lack of regulated standards and approved practices like the generally accepted accounting practices (GAAP) of the accounting field. Standards such as GAAP establish a level of standards for industries so that many people can prescribe actions and interpret results according to the same set of expectations. When it comes to management in the new economy, the lack of licensing and regulation makes defining ebusiness competencies extremely difficult.

In the absence of comprehensive skill measurement, some managers mistakenly assume that an employee with *some* level of experience with digital activities implies adequate skill. Putting personnel in posi- tions for which they are not qualified can be of potential detriment. In terms of ebusiness initiatives, though, there is a more common and dan- gerous management tendency than putting personnel in positions for which they are unqualified. Since most digital activities require the use of technology, many managers tend to place an overemphasis on technical requirements such as technical personnel certifications and hardware specifications. While such issues are certainly of high importance, they can easily detract from equally critical components of ebusiness execution. While digital competency does require a high level of technical expertise, this is only a portion of what's required for ebusiness success.

To compete successfully in the digital arena, managers need to enlist personnel with expertise in the three vital areas, briefly introduced earlier in Chapter 2. The first, technical skill, is the ability to appropriately use and manage technical resources such as hardware, software, data, and telecommunications infrastructure. The second, people skill, is the ability to influence stakeholders to carry out ebusiness activities. The third, conceptual skill, is the ability to see the organization as a whole and understand the impact of ebusiness activities on the objectives of the organization. These three areas of skill comprise the competencies necessary to achieve ebusiness success.

Technical Skill

Technical skill is extremely important in designing and implementing ebusiness initiatives. By default, this area typically receives the most attention from managers because technology is the baseline component of all digital activities. Whether a company is considering a new Web site application or developing a data collection tool on a Palm Pilot, technology is at the core of the activity. Frankly, the technical area is often considered especially vital because the reliability and availability of systems have become a major prerequisite to the success of ebusiness initiatives. If the hardware, software, and connectivity of systems are not functional, the initiatives they are intended to support are simply not viable.

Individuals who possess technical skill are varied in background and area of involvement. Areas of technical expertise range from network maintenance and server administration to Web site design and database production. Technical experts include those personnel who directly handle technology—for example, PC support technicians. Other technical experts include those who manage technical personnel—for instance, MIS directors and chief information officers. These personnel are vital to digital activities because they develop, enhance, and maintain the systems upon which digital activities take place.

People Skill

While technical expertise is certainly critical to the success of digital activities, equally important is the focus that others lend to the usability of digital applications by the organization's stakeholders. Managers must pay special attention to the compatibility of technical systems with those for whom they have been designed. Microsoft is an organization that is particularly in tune with this issue. Through its accessibility program, Microsoft invests heavily into ensuring that technology is available to those with disabilities. Microsoft recognizes that even the most innovative technologies are useless unless accessible to and compatible with all users. Some systems are either too confusing or too difficult for individuals to use. The technology might be perfectly functional but rendered useless if not friendly to all types of users. What is needed here is people skill, the second area of necessary expertise.

Defined in the context of digital dimensioning, people skill is the ability to understand and direct digital activities toward the best interests of stakeholders. People skill is critical in ensuring that digital activities mesh with the needs and capabilities of users. Those with people skill typically have a down-to-earth personality and possess a keen insight or awareness regarding the needs and feelings of others. People experts are sensitive to the individual and collective needs of human beings. People skill is extremely important in the digital dimensioning process because it aids organizations in considering the impact that digital activities have on their constituents. Put simply, enlisting people skill helps to ensure that digital technology is easily accessible to internal and external customers.

When participating in the digital dimensioning process, those with people skill play the vital role of advocating customer convenience and usability. To repeat a point made earlier, the most efficient of technologies are essentially useless if not readily accessible and usable by the intended audience. From the employee who wants to access the organization's intranet to the customer who wants to check the status of a recent online order, digital applications must be conveniently and easily accessible. Individuals who possess people skill vary by position in an organization. Those with the most people skill can range from the frontline receptionist to human resources officers. While many organizations have designated positions to assist in issues of human relationships, those with people skill can exist in any or every area of an organization. Technical skill and people skill, when working together, can ensure that digital applications are not only functional, but accessible as well.

Conceptual Skill

Assuming that technology is working in concert with internal and external customers, the next concern is that of the organization as a whole. Digital activities must be conducted with the broad goals and objectives of the organization. Managers must be sure to include those personnel who are mindful of the impact that digital activities have on the organization. The third area of skill critical to the digital dimensioning process is conceptual skill. This area of expertise involves the ability to see all parts of the organization as a unified whole contributing to goal attainment. This might include activities related to an organization's external environment such as competitor analysis and consumer research. It also includes activities regarding an organization's internal environment such as process development and management training. Another key aspect of the conceptual skill area embraces the financial considerations of the organization. Digital activities must be planned and implemented according to the financial position of the organization. At the very least, a fundamental knowledge of financial mechanics and tactics helps to ensure that digital activities are financially feasible and grounded in a potential return on investment. Conceptual experts are essentially advocates and watchdogs of the organization as a whole. They consider the economic impact of digital activities and should be involved to keep digital activities directed toward goal attainment and profitability. They are able to scrutinize an effort in terms of the potential revenue wrought, costs saved, or services enhanced.

Conceptual skill is often present in various areas of an organization. Many organizations have traditionally depended on senior managers to generate and refine conceptual strategies. Organizations operating in the new economy, however, depend on all levels of an organization for conceptual skill and thinking. Competitiveness in the new economy often demands the conceptual awareness and contribution of many, if not all, organizational members.

Putting Them Together

Conceptual skill, complemented by technical skill and people skill, contributes to a sound balance of the appropriate skill necessary in designing, implementing, and managing digital activities. If managers have these skills available, the chances for ebusiness success are significantly increased. Determining the presence of particular skills, though, is often a subjective practice. There are certification test scores measuring tech-

nical skill, personality inventories to gauge people skill, and past performance appraisals to assess conceptual skill; however, there is an
absence of proven metric tools to help managers determine the level of
such skills in the context of ebusiness.

Assessing Digital Dimensioning Skills

Managers must certainly understand the three components of digital
dimensioning skill and what role each plays in creating collective digital
expertise. Beyond definition, though, a manager must also grasp the successive degrees of each skill area: The presence of *some* degree of skill
in a given skill area does not ensure that there is an adequate degree of
skill. For the purposes of digital dimensioning, managers can gauge the
degrees of technical, people, and conceptual skill relatively accurately. In
lieu of widely accepted skill inventories, managers can assess skill level
by simply exploring the degree of employees' capabilities based upon
their demonstration of such. Each skill area should be carefully considered before determining if personnel possess it. Managers need to assess
the degree of those individual skills prior to labeling someone an expert.
For example, just because a person has built a personal Web page during her free time does not necessarily mean that she has the adequate
technical skill necessary to participate in all digital dimensioning activities. Additionally, an employee who does all of her shopping on the Web
does not necessarily understand the complexities of developing an
appropriate online business model and may not necessarily possess the
conceptual skill required for all digital dimensioning activities.

While these examples illustrate seemingly obvious pitfalls, many
managers fall into them. Managers make the mistake of assuming that
personnel who have *any* background with the Internet should be and
are appropriate to be involved with ongoing digital initiatives. It is
important to note that awareness, surface knowledge, or even experience does not necessarily correlate to appropriate digital expertise in
the context of an organization. It is not adequate to enlist a person
because he or she possesses *some* skill. Managers must enlist those personnel with *enough* skill. Each of the three skill areas—people, technical, and conceptual—can be segmented into different levels. Each of
these levels can be assessed according to a simple metric approach that
helps management explore the degree of a person's skill. Skill levels are
quantified on a scale of 1 to 5, with 1 representing a low level of skill
and 5 representing a high level. Managers can evaluate a person's skill

level by comparing the person's general faculties, experience, and performance with the attributes associated with each skill level.

The levels and attributes of each skill area are sorted into separate tables, giving managers the ability to quickly assess a person's skill. As each table is presented, it will be explained to provide specific insight into the individual considerations and nuances inherent in that table of skills.

Keep in mind that the purpose of describing skill level is to give managers an understanding of the spectrum of skill levels. Therefore, a table should be used in the context of a working reference tool, not a diagnostic assessment survey. At the same time, there are certainly many skill levels above and below those listed in the tables. For example, the technical skill levels listed in Table 3.1 indicate that a person who is proficient in desktop applications has a low skill level. However, in some organizational situations a person with such characteristics could easily be considered very technically savvy. For the purposes of digital dimensioning, though, many of the technical requirements far exceed skill attributes like word processing. Simply keep in mind that there are skill levels that precede and exceed those in the tables.

Degrees of Technical Skill

It is especially important to evaluate an individual's technical skill before entrusting that individual with large technical responsibilities. Oftentimes, managers who do not have much technical knowledge automatically assume that those organization members who are generally "good with computers" are capable of developing Web applications or other associated activities. However, a look at the technical skills in Table 3.1 shows that a person with a very strong working knowledge of common desktop applications actually has a relatively low technical skill level in terms of digital dimensioning. It is therefore critical that managers understand that digital dimensioning activities may require significantly more technical expertise than currently exists within their organizations.

Degrees of People Skill

The second skill area, people skill, certainly has varying skill degrees as well. Overall the varying levels of people skill correlate to an individual's insight into personal and team mechanics. Ranging from a basic understanding of internal and external customer needs to a full grasp of customer service strategies, the varying degrees of people skill are definitive and gradual. Table 3.2 contains a successive list of people skill degrees.

Table 3.1   Successive degrees of technical skill for digital activities.

Skill Level	Technical Skill Attribute
1	Can effectively utilize common desktop applications such as a word processor
2	Can effectively utilize specialized software applications such as graphics, database, and engineering tools
3	Can perform basic programming tasks such as building static Web pages or modifying existing ones
4	Can perform complex programming tasks such as building dynamic Web applications or developing data-driven tools
5	Can create and implement comprehensive software and database applications such as ERP systems or deeply technical Web applications

Table 3.2   Successive degrees of people skill for digital activities.

Skill Level	People Skill Attribute
1	Understands the basic needs of customers (internal and external)
2	Possesses general insight into improving the organization's ability to meet customer needs
3	Understands competitive factors relating to meeting customer needs
4	Understands and considers the psychological and emotional implications of current and modified customer service activities
5	Can create and modify customer service strategies according to the psychological and emotional considerations of customers

Degrees of Conceptual Skill

Conceptual skill also has varying degrees as well. This is perhaps the most difficult skill level to understand and appreciate. Many managers tend to evaluate conceptual skill intuitively. In some cases, personal intuition about a person's conceptual skill is very important, and in many cases, critical. Bruce Carpenter, senior vice president of Fiserv, CBS

Worldwide, observes personal attributes of personnel as part of evaluating the person's ability to think conceptually. Overall strategic competence depends in part on the things people do to equip themselves with prowess. One such attribute that Carpenter examines is the issue of perpetual self-education. As fast as the commercial Internet landscape is growing and evolving, one must be ever mindful of new trends and considerations as a part of thinking strategically. Types of trends include shifts in customer tendencies and developments in legislative policy. The only way to be aware of such trends is to proactively search for them in the right periodicals, Web sites, television programs, and other news sources. According to Carpenter, those who have a hunger for information are naturally valuable to conceptual discussion. The presence of attributes like self-study can be an effective indicator in evaluating conceptual skill. Overall, though, the conceptual skill table can be an insightful guide in understanding the spectrum of this skill area. Table 3.3 shows the varying degrees of conceptual skill.

Table 3.3 Successive degrees of conceptual skill for digital activities.

Skill Level	Conceptual Skill Attribute
1	Understands the organization's overall purpose
2	Understands the organization's mission, goals, and objectives
3	Understands the internal and external forces involved in developing and refining the organization's ongoing strategy
4	Understands various business models relative to traditional and online norms and trends
5	Can develop and refine various models according to commercial trends and can develop implementation paths consistent with measurable return on investment

Assessing the Skill Requirements of Digital Activities

Once a manager understands the skill types and degrees involved in the digital dimensioning process, the focus then shifts to determining the types of skills and degrees required for various digital activities. In

Figure 3.1, this step is illustrated in box 2. Since different types of digital activities require different types and levels of technical, conceptual, and people skill, it is common to involve various personnel in different projects. For example, the technical skills needed to publish a piece of employee literature on the Web are much different from those technical skills required to build a business application for a handheld device. Because of the difference in skill levels required for various digital activities, there is no single prescription that dictates which people to involve on *all* digital projects. Due to the varying needs of the different projects, managers must understand how to assess the skill requirements of each project and the skill degrees of the different personnel.

The three skill tables are important because they suggest different levels of skill to managers. The different levels of skill give managers a clear understanding of how much skill an individual might have. But how does a manager decide which level of skill is necessary for a given project? Which digital activities require high levels of skill versus low? There is no definitive answer to such questions, but there certainly are clear examples of common digital activities and the general skill requirements of each. One such activity might be the maintenance of press material on an established Web site. This activity requires a relatively low skill level in comparison to other digital activities. Developing comprehensive online customer service strategies, for example, requires very high levels of skill.

Table 3.4 contains a column of common digital activities followed by a column for each of the three skill areas. In each of the skill columns is a number or range of numbers correlating to the amount of that skill required to successfully complete the corresponding activity. For example, developing broad Internet strategies, a common digital activity, requires a relatively high level of each skill, whereas maintaining Web site content, another digital activity, requires very low levels of each skill. The table's intent is to give managers an understanding of how much skill in each of the three areas is generally required for each activity. As indicated earlier, it is critical that management assigns personnel with the appropriate skills to participate in various digital activities. This table should serve as a helpful guide in locating the appropriate personnel. Keep in mind that the table contains only a handful of sample activities. Other digital activities have varying requirements that can be determined through a working knowledge of this table.

Table 3.4 Common digital activities and their skill-level requirements.

Digital Activity	Technical	Conceptual	People
Developing broad Internet strategies	4–5	5	5
Refining Web site aesthetics	2–3	4–5	5
Maintaining Web site content	1–3	1	1–2
Evaluating and implementing enterprise software solutions	5	4–5	4–5
Developing Internet marketing strategies	3–5	5	5
Building online customer surveys	3–4	4	4–5
Revamping the company intranet	4–5	5	5
Selecting computer hardware vendors	5	1	1–2

Identifying Expertise: Surveying the Organization for Required Skills

After managers have a firm understanding of both the multiple skills involved in the digital dimensioning process and the varying skill requirements of different digital activities, the next task is to actually examine the organization for the presence of required skills. This step—enlisting digital expertise—is shown in box 3 of Figure 3.1. In some organizations, all of the skills exist and are readily available to management. In most organizations, however, one or more are either not present or not available. Thus, the result of examining the organization for the presence of available and sufficiently degreed skills can yield one of three possibilities, as shown in boxes 3a, 3b, and 3c of Figure 3.1

1. All Required Skills Are Present Internally

In many cases, all required degrees of technical, people, and conceptual skill are both present within the organization and available to participate in digital dimensioning activities (box 3a of Figure 3.1). Under this set of circumstances, management can simply call on those personnel with the appropriate expertise to participate in the digital dimensioning process.

2. Some Required Skills Are Present Internally

In other instances, management may find that only *some* of the skills required for digital activities are present and available within the organization (box 3b of Figure 3.1). When this occurs, managers have two options. The first option is to train insufficiently skilled personnel to the required skill level. The second option is to acquire external expertise in the form of new hires or outside consultants. Regardless of which option is most attractive, managers must take steps to supplement skilled internal personnel in one or more skill areas.

3. No Required Skills Are Present Internally

The third possible outcome of an organizational search for digital dimensioning skills is that *no* required skills are present within the organization (box 3c of Figure 3.1). Like the circumstance of finding *some* skill within the organization, the manager's fundamental challenge when finding *no* skills within the organization is to bring sufficient levels of skill into the digital dimensioning process. The manager can accomplish this by training internal personnel or locating outside expertise in one or more skill areas. However, while training employees may be ideal in many instances, it can take a significant amount of time to accomplish. When time is of the essence, managers may choose to look for sources of expertise outside the organization.

External Expertise

External expertise is commonly utilized by many organizations when internal expertise is not sufficient or available. For the most part, external expertise exists in the form of individual consultants or consulting firms. Each of the three skill areas is present in a variety of forms within these entities. Some individual consultants may specialize in various technical areas of skill, for example. Since there is such a broad array of digital activities, many tend to specialize in a particular operating system or development arena. Other sources of external expertise provide a variety of skills. Some consulting firms, for instance, have high levels of technical, conceptual, and people skill readily available for various client engagements. Examples of such companies include Razorfish, iXL, and Scient. Such companies offer a wide selection of digital activities including online branding, ebusiness strategy, Web site development, and ecommerce. Some specialize in various digital arenas.

Razorfish, for example, has a special area of practice that focuses on wireless application development. A visitor who enters the Razorfish office in Manhattan can order and pay for a soft drink from the lobby's soda machine using a wireless phone. Visitors call the telephone number on the machine, which dispenses the selected product and bills the transaction to the customer's cellular account. Razorfish is pushing its clients to the edge of digital technology by thinking outside the box and embodying a companywide culture of digital vision and foresight.

External digital dimensioning expertise comes in various shapes and sizes. A wealth of expertise can be found within a host of independent contractors. The benefits of technology combined with the new rules of a changing economy have created an entire population of "free agent" workers who are simply individual consultants with a wide range of expertise and experience. They opt to work for a host of organizational clients for varying lengths of times as opposed to working for a single employer. Free agents can be identified and contacted through a variety of vehicles. Word-of-mouth referrals are usually a good source for finding viable consultants. Web sites such as Guru.com serve as a central repository for individual consulting talent for hire.

Individual consultants can serve a number of needs for organizations. Many assist in specialized areas of technical skill. Some consultants are specially trained in a particular software package or coding language. Their assistance is more production-oriented because they spend time building software or maintaining systems. Others, who have experience with a specific type of business situation, work with organizations to negotiate the same type of circumstance. Their assistance is more concept-oriented because they spend time developing and refining strategies. Whatever skill is needed, individual consultants are a viable route toward locating specialized expertise suitable for specific requirements.

Another form of external expertise is that of consulting and production firms. Consulting firms contain teams of personnel who can meet the skill needs of clients. These firms exist in a wide varity of forms and sizes to serve various organizations with varying needs. Implementation companies like Inforte, for example, specialize in implementing third-party software products for larger ebusinesses. Interactive agencies such as Organic Online specialize in developing online brand identities and deploy Web sites for mass consumer marketing. Management consulting firms such as Accenture assist organizations in developing online business models and monitoring competition. Systems providers such as IBM provide clients with hardware, software, and installation services. As these examples indicate, there is a broad spectrum of consulting firms that contain external skills.

For many organizations, a primary challenge in assembling adequate expertise is simply admitting that outside resources are either more qualified or more readily available than internal resources, which are typically used by default. When managers are willing to explore external resources that might possess necessary skills, the opportunities for rapid execution are many. Mismanaging the selection and supervision of outside resources, though, can be very costly and counterproductive. After making the decision to enlist external expertise, management must be diligent in exploring and reviewing the fitness of such resources in accord with the present needs of the organization. Experienced consultants and contractors will usually have a portfolio of relevant experience to help management measure the presence and degree of relevant skills. Instead of relying completely on a consultant's self-representation, it is an accepted (and important) practice to speak with some of the consultant's existing or former clients as reference sources. The nature and degree of a consultant's technical expertise can be assessed by checking on background project experience. If prudently selected, external expertise can add significant value to digital efforts.

Organizing and Mobilizing Digital Expertise

Once managers locate sources of expertise inside and/or outside an organization, the final step in enlisting expertise is organizing and mobilizing those experts. This step is shown in box 4 of Figure 3.1. When combining internal and external expertise, the nature and qualifications of the different skill sets are such that different personnel from various organizational departments are likely to be involved in digital activities. It would not be uncommon, for example, for a software engineer in an organization's IT department who possesses technical skill to work with a communications expert from the marketing department who possesses conceptual skill. The overwhelming majority of digital activities require skills from various departments within an organization. In fact, it would be very rare that *all* necessary skills for a project would be found within one branch of the organization.

Given this tendency, the premise of assembling the appropriate expertise rests upon a cross-functional mentality. Each digital initiative, be it a micro Web site for a new product or a new extranet feature for suppliers, requires the synthesis of diverse organizational components. Many digital activities can be gathered together into areas of specialty so that cross-functional teams can work together on a number of digital activities within a group. One team might work on all wireless projects, while another might handle all Web-based projects. Whatever the case, these teams will more than likely take a cross-functional approach.

There are inherent challenges in this type of team structure, though. Of these challenges, three are typical. First, people from different areas of an organization are not always familiar with the working styles of one another. Similar to athletic teams, members of cross-functional teams need time to get to know one another and gel together. As they do become familiar with each other, positive working relationships and creative synergy are likely to emerge. Cross-functional teams can even develop their own culture and identity as an instrument of building and reinforcing the team mentality.

Creating a strong bond between cross-functional team members is not always practical in this sense, though. In some cases, competition among various company divisions can create a dysfunctional team character. Team members tend to focus more on the intangible issues of credit and authority as opposed to the actual objectives of the team. Managers must carefully monitor the evolution of team relationships and continually reward those individuals who commit energy toward achieving the team's goals.

The second challenge of a cross-functional approach rests in the varying geographies that separate team members. Internal personnel from different departments might be on separate floors, in different buildings, or even in various time zones. External expertise is almost always located off-site from the organization's physical location. In these cases, special effort must be made to ensure that the "out-of-sight, out-of-mind" mentality does not prevent a digital initiative from moving forward.

When team initiatives are driven by people and resources in various locations, the challenges can be quite daunting. For starters, tasks and action items tend to be placed on the back burner because of firsthand issues that seem more pressing. At the same time, communicating and collaborating over large distances and across time zones takes away the benefits and synergy of face-to-face collaboration. In terms of the challenges presented by geographic separation, managers must take appropriate steps to soften the negative impact of these circumstances. First, be sure that the superiors of the team members are on board with and aware of the team's initiatives. This will enable the superiors to hold their team members accountable to team activities and performance. In turn, the team members will treat team initiatives not as back-burner enrichment activities, but as very tangible activities associated with job performance. Second, encourage as many face-to-face meetings as possible. Schedule groups of meetings at a time to ensure that valuable team resources are not spent on determining meeting times week after week. These simple steps should help to address the challenges of geographic distances.

Yet a third challenge of cross-functional collaboration and team structure rests in the elements of authority and accountability. Since cross-functional teams transcend traditional organization structure, it is often unclear how team member performance is measured and who reviews and evaluates performance. When structuring cross-functional teams, it is notably important that performance criteria and expectations are determined and measured. At the same time, it is critical that the responsibility of team performance and success is assigned to a team's leader.

The challenges of cross-functional collaboration are many. Managers must certainly be conscious of such challenges and address those that might have a negative impact on a digital initiative. But there are also a number of positive attributes of a cross-functional approach to digital projects. If managers are able to capitalize on the positive attributes of cross-functional collaboration and minimize the impact of the negative ones, the chances of success are greatly improved.

The primary positive attribute is the team's broad organizational perspective. Since a truly cross-functional approach is likely to bring the perspectives of several departments, the net team perspective is likely to include many different views of organizational challenges and opportunities. This diverse composition should be a more accurate view of the organization as opposed to the limited one that is often wrought by the inclusion of only one or two departments. Digital dimensioning activities need the perspective of the *whole* organization, not just individual facets.

Digital activities are often very complex in nature and scope. There are a host of variables that team members must consider. Every facet of a project—from software and hardware choices to fundamentally differing business model alternatives—presents teams with challenging decisions. The pressures of Internet speed and competition make decisions about such variables very critical. The expertise and wisdom found in the diversity of cross-functional groups is vital to sound decision making. But since this diversity can also be a hindrance to a team's efforts, it is most important that managers take advantage of the positives and minimize the negatives when creating and structuring cross-functional teams.

Digital expertise is the life force of the digital dimensioning process. Because of its significance, "enlisting digital expertise" is the first and foremost step of the process itself. Even the best laid plans can succumb to failure if properly skilled internal and external expertise is not put into place. In exploring further aspects of the digital dimensioning process, be ever mindful of perhaps the most critical component: skilled personnel.

Back to Fiserv

The purpose of this section is to illustrate how chapter principles apply to the situation at Fiserv. The following is a reflection of advice that a consultant might have given Fiserv in an effort to engage the appropriate personnel in the digital dimensioning process.

"When determining which people to involve in the ebusiness-related projects or activities, first consider the skills required for success. While technical skill is certainly critical, be mindful of the importance of people skill and conceptual skill in developing solutions that are not only functional but user friendly for customers and beneficial to the organization as well. When evaluating employees who might potentially participate, be sure to evaluate not just the presence of skill but the degree of skill as well. If it is determined that the required skills are either not all present or not available within an organization, a viable alternative is that of external consultants and contractors. External skill comes in many sizes and configurations. Because of this, be sure to match requirements with appropriate contractors in order to ensure success. Selected internal and external expertise will naturally result in a diverse and cross-functional team. Because this circumstance has both negative and positive implications, be sure to minimize the negative effects and maximize the positive ones."

Digital Dimensioning Resolutions

- Appreciate the value of human capital to organizational success.

- Carefully consider the nature of the three digital dimensioning skill areas.

- Explore the entire organization for the presence of people, conceptual, and technical skill.

- Ensure that organizational members have the appropriate amount of skill required by digital activities.

- If the appropriate skill is not present within the organization, look to outside resources for assistance.

- Be sure not to overemphasize the importance of any one skill area.

- Design teams of personnel with a cross-functional mentality.

- Be aware of the potential pitfalls of cross-functional teams.

- Understand the advantages of cross-functional teams.

- Attempt to maximize the advantages and minimize the disadvantages of the cross-functional approach to teams.

- Take practical steps to assemble digital expertise in accord with organizational objectives.

chapter 4

Analyzing the Digital Environment

Executive Preview

This chapter discusses how to analyze an organization's digital environment. Discussion begins by defining an organization's digital environment and explaining *why* managers must carefully analyze and understand the digital environment. The chapter depicts the digital environment as consisting of three levels: general, operating, and internal. Special attention is given to the significance of each level within the analysis process. The chapter also describes various sources of information for analyzing an organization's digital environment. An important part of the chapter explains how managers can use SWOT analysis to make sense of diverse information gathered during the analysis of a digital environment. It also gives advice for improving how an organization analyzes its digital environment. The chapter opens with a discussion of General Electric's posture of adopting useful Internet applications in all business units and draws to a close with digital dimensioning advice that a consultant could have given General Electric's managers as input for initiating ebusiness applications. The chapter ends with resolutions that you can make to enhance the ebusiness competitiveness of *your* organization.

GE Pushes Ebusiness in Each Business Unit[1]

General Electric (GE) is one of the largest industrial corporations in the world. GE manufactures a seemingly endless array of products, including home appliances, lighting products, medical diagnostic imaging equipment, and commercial and military aircraft jet engines. Also, through its National Broadcasting Company, Inc., GE delivers network television services, operates television stations, and provides cable programming.

GE is very well known for its aggressiveness in employing ebusiness strategies and tactics. General Electric's chairman and CEO, Jack Welch, strongly encourages each business unit to use ebusiness applications wherever possible. In addition, Welch supports the notion that managers in each business unit should determine how the Internet could help grow their business and then develop strategies to implement their ideas.

One noteworthy Internet application at GE has come in the home appliances area. Initially, management seemed to support the idea of selling home appliances directly to consumers via the Internet. However, extended data gathering and related deliberation led management to the conclusion that a significant portion of GE's appliances, like refrigerators and cooking stoves, were sold through chain stores that could retaliate against GE's selling directly to consumers by pushing competing brands. So GE revised its idea to use the Internet, instead, to improve the process of selling appliances to chain stores. As a result, at least two-thirds of Home Depot's stores have been connected to GE's new Web-based order and delivery system. The new system is aimed at improving GE's sales process and delivery system. The stores benefit through more efficient and reliable ordering. At least for now, GE does not favor selling its appliances directly to consumers.

Principles for Analyzing the Digital Environment

What's Ahead? The Spotlight emphasized Jack Welch's orientation of encouraging Internet applications throughout GE's business units. The company's decision to forgo selling directly to consumers and to build better systems between GE and its retail business partners is noteworthy. The message is clear: Making the wrong decision about employing ebusiness strategies and tactics can alienate stakeholders in an organization's digital environment and thereby hinder organizational success. What is unclear, however, is exactly how to analyze the digital environment so that such misapplications of ebusiness can be avoided. This chapter focuses on how to analyze an organization's digital environment.

Analyzing the Digital Environment: What and Why

Digital environment is defined as the set of factors, both outside and inside the organization, that can affect digital performance. Examples of such factors include the level of competition for product sales, economic unrest and uncertainty, and existing relationships with suppliers.

Analyzing the digital environment is the process of assessing an organization's digital surroundings to identify strengths, weaknesses, opportunities, and threats that can serve as a foundation for determining the digital direction that an organization should pursue. "Analyzing the digital environment" is the second step of the digital dimensioning process. The success of every organization's digital efforts is subject to the influence of a broad range of outside factors. In essence, an organization's digital success or failure depends on how accurately its managers define the digital environment and how appropriately they respond to it. Without appropriate adaptation to its digital environment, the digital presence of an organization will likely fail to achieve desired results.

Know the Structure of the Digital Environment

Analyzing an organization's digital environment seems impossible without a thorough understanding of what constitutes that environment. In essence, what is the basic structure of the digital environment? This book proposes a model of an organization's digital environment that has three distinct levels: general, operating, and internal. Figure 4.1 shows the relationship of each of these levels with the others and with the organization itself. The figure also shows the various components that make up each level.

This model of the digital environment is *not* intended as a complete, accurate description of the digital environment of every organization. Instead, the model represents a logical construct for describing a generic digital environment. Managers should modify this model to represent

Figure 4.1 The digital environment.

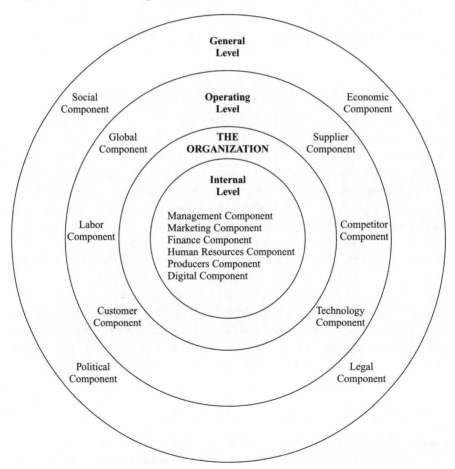

the components of their particular organizations. In studying this generic model, managers should scrutinize the three digital environmental levels, know what factors they include, and try to understand how each factor and the relationships among them affect digital direction. Once managers understand the generic environmental structure, they can modify the number of environmental levels and even components in each environmental level to suit unique organizational circumstances. The following sections describe the generic model in detail.

The General Level

The *general level* is that level of an organization's digital environment that is outside the organization, has components that are relatively slow in changing, and tends to impact digital direction relatively slowly over time. What are the components of the general level?

The *economic component* of the general level focuses on the distribution and uses of resources within an entire society. Examples of factors within the economic component include the inflation rate, employment rate, interest rates, tax rates, and consumer income, debt, and spending patterns. These factors are important to digital planning because, in large part, they can impact critical issues like the size, scope, and success of an organization's digital thrust.

In addition to the traditional economic issues such as those stated above, this component also includes issues related to the so-called Internet economy. This economy is indeed substantial. A recent issue of *Computer Dealer News* indicated that the U.S. Internet economy supported an additional 650,000 jobs in 1999 and in 2000 supported 2.476 million workers. That's more workers than are supported by the insurance industry, the communications industry, and the public utilities industry. Additionally, that's twice as many workers as supported by the airline industry, the chemical industry, and the legal and real estate industries. Some of the Internet-related jobs were newly created, while others reflect companies shifting workers to take advantage of opportunities in the Internet economy. Monitoring the progress of this Internet economy would be very useful for managers attempting to establish digital direction. Almost every existing industry will be competing in the future with the Internet economy for needed human resources.

The *social component* of the digital environment's general level describes characteristics of the society or societies in which the organization exists. Society issues like literacy rates, familiarity with technology, education levels, customs, beliefs, values, lifestyles, population age distribution, and the mobility of the population all contribute to this social component. Inevitably, such dimensions of a society significantly impact the character and success of digital efforts within that society. Obviously, analyzing the social component of the general level can be extremely challenging. Analyzing multiple societies becomes even more complex and challenging.

The *political component* of the general level relates to government affairs. This component includes government attitudes toward various digital industries, lobbying efforts by various interest groups, the overall regulatory climate, digital platform components of political parties, and even predispositions of candidates for office. Political issues can be precursors to the types of pressure and influence that will eventually impact the digital thrust in organizations.

As an example of how the political component might influence planning for digital activities, at this time the federal government seems to strongly support the notion that digital activities represent a new opportunity for providing higher productivity and a higher standard of living. Although at this time the political arena overall seems strongly inclined to encourage the conscientious growth of the Internet, some issues, such as taxing Internet sales or safeguarding Internet user privacy, may run counter to the interests of some organizations and cause them to lobby lawmakers.

The *legal component* of the general level consists of laws that members of society are expected to follow. Understandably, the very early years of the Internet resembled a lawless society and a new frontier. However, things have begun to change very quickly. As an example, consider copyright law as it relates to the Internet. Early on, there was considerable uncertainty about the application of intellectual property law as it related to placing material on the Internet. More recently, the fundamental principles of copyright, trademark, and patent have been upheld in the courts as applying to Internet communication and commerce. In the early 1990s significant uncertainty existed regarding the utility of traditional copyright laws as protection for authored works in the digital environment. Today, however, it is now clear that traditional copyright law fully protects material appearing on the Internet. Court decisions clearly prohibit the unauthorized online transmission of copyrighted work

To a significant extent, the number of future ebusiness laws is determined by feedback that legislators receive about ebusiness activity. For example, in 1999 the Federal Trade Commission received more than 18,000 ebusiness complaints, more than double the previous year's volume. This trend is expected to continue. Additionally, according to a recent study by the Computer Security Institute and the FBI, cyberattacks on companies are increasing significantly. Nearly 300 of the companies studied reported losses of more than $265 million due to cyberattacks. Such attacks have rendered organizations like CNN.com, Microsoft, Buy.com, and eBay unable to provide service to customers for extended periods of time.

Due at least partially to such feedback, legislative bodies throughout the world seem to be establishing Internet laws of various kinds with blistering speed. The state legislature of Florida is an example of a legislative body moving quickly in this area. Florida's 2000 legislative session was marked by the passage of a mammoth ecommerce bill. The bill includes tax incentives for high-tech businesses, makes electronic documents as legitimate as their paper counterparts, and requires government agencies to accept them. When Governor Jeb Bush signed the measure, he called it the most comprehensive, all-encompassing technology reform in Florida's history.

The Operating Level

The *operating level* is that level of the organization's digital environment that is outside the organization, has components that are relatively quick in changing, and tends to impact digital direction relatively quickly. As Figure 4.1 indicates, the major components of the operating environment are customers, competitors, technology, labor, suppliers, and global issues.

The *customer component* of the digital environment's operating level reflects the characteristics and behavior of those who buy the organization's goods and services. Describing in detail those who buy the firm's products is a common business practice. Such customer profiles can help management generate ideas about establishing digital direction that can improve areas like customer relations and satisfaction.

Much effort is continually being spent on trying to understand online customers. In the future, more and more Internet users are expected to shop online. A recent study by ACNeilsen indicated that 48 percent of those who visit the Internet purchase products or services online. The report also indicates that although the number of men and women using the Internet is now nearly identical, the number of women using and purchasing on the Internet has been on the rise in the last several years. The study refers to the group that logs on to the Internet daily as "heavy users," the group that accesses the Internet several times a week as "medium users," and the group that only visits the Internet once a week as "light users." Males tend to be heavy users and females tend to be light users. The majority of all users access the Internet from home. Information of this nature about online customers can be invaluable for a manager attempting to understand an organization's digital environment.

The *competitor component* of the digital environment's operating level consists of rivals that an organization must overcome in order to reach its objectives. Understanding competitors is a key factor in developing digital direction, and a prerequisite for digital success. Overall, competitor analysis is intended to help management know the competition and thereby be better armed to employ the digital direction needed to best compete.

The *labor component* of the digital environment's operating level is made up of influences on the supply of workers available to perform needed organizational tasks. This component includes issues that are important to the operation of the organization, such as potential employee skill levels, wage rates, and average ages of potential workers. Managers often overlook another important labor-related issue: the attractiveness of working for a particular organization, as perceived by potential workers. Analyzing the labor component will help management generate ideas about establishing digital direction that will ensure that the organization has needed human resources.

The *supplier component* of the digital environment's operating level includes the influence of providers of resources to the organization. The firm purchases and transforms these resources during the production process into final goods and services. The number of vendors that offer specified resources for sale, the relative quality of materials they offer, the reliability of their deliveries, and the credit terms they offer are all sample issues included in this component. Analyzing suppliers helps management generate ideas about establishing digital direction that enhances the overall contribution that suppliers make to the organization.

The *technology component* of the digital environment's operating level includes new approaches to producing goods and services—new procedures *and* new equipment. This component includes digital as well as all other organizationally related technology. An example of a more traditionally monitored factor in this component is the use of robots to improve productivity. An example of a factor that has begun to be monitored in more recent times is the use of wireless technology in delivering digital services. Overall, analyzing the technology component helps management generate ideas about establishing digital direction that assists in best employing technology.

The *global component* of the digital environment's operating level includes all factors related to an organization's operations in foreign countries. Significant global component issues include the laws, language, political practices, cultures, and economic climates that prevail in the countries in which the firm does business. In these times when the world seems to be getting smaller and smaller, management's clear understanding of the global component seems to be of paramount importance. Knowing this global component will help managers determine the digital directions to best facilitate global operations.

Dealing with foreign laws that impact digital activities is a highly publicized challenge facing modern managers. One high-profile example involves Yahoo and the People's Republic of China. Looking to expand globally, Yahoo management recently decided to launch a Yahoo China Web site. Yahoo planned Yahoo China as a joint venture with Founder, a newspaper publisher and software developer. The joint venture, however, hit a significant snag. The problem seemed to stem from significant "gray areas" within China's Internet laws. Thoroughly understanding the global component of the digital environment's operating level in such situations can avoid costly digital slowdowns or mistakes.

The Internal Level

The *internal level* is that level of the organization's digital environment that is inside the organization, has components that tend to change quickly, and tends to impact digital direction quickly. Figure 4.2 illustrates the digital environment's internal level, its major components, and sample issues for each component.

The *management component* is that segment of the internal level of an organization's digital environment that houses all the factors dealing with planning, organizing, influencing, and controlling. The communication network established to allow interaction among organization members, the structure of the organization with established authority and responsibility relationships in the organization, and organizational goals are all major issues within the management component. Obviously, many other management issues are also part of the manage-

Figure 4.2 Major components of the internal environment and sample issues included in each.

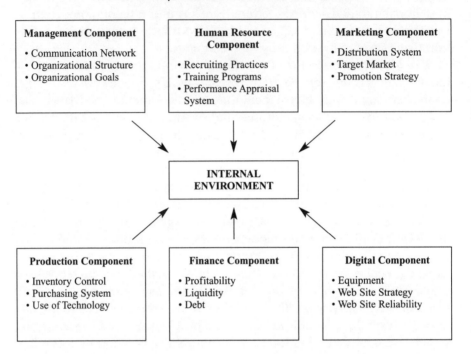

Management Component	**Human Resource Component**	**Marketing Component**
• Communication Network • Organizational Structure • Organizational Goals	• Recruiting Practices • Training Programs • Performance Appraisal System	• Distribution System • Target Market • Promotion Strategy

INTERNAL ENVIRONMENT

Production Component	**Finance Component**	**Digital Component**
• Inventory Control • Purchasing System • Use of Technology	• Profitability • Liquidity • Debt	• Equipment • Web Site Strategy • Web Site Reliability

ment component. Information describing management activities in an organization provide the basis for using digital thrust to complement organizational management.

The *production component* is that segment of the internal level of an organization's digital environment that houses all the factors dealing with the organizational process used to produce goods and services. Issues here include, but are not limited to, controlling inventory, using technology in the production process, and procuring materials needed for the production process. Information describing production, and activity related to production, in an organization serves as the foundation for ideas about using digital thrust to improve production.

The *finance component* is that segment of the internal level of an organization's digital environment that houses factors related to the financial condition of the organization. Issues here include, but are not limited to, the profitability of the organization, the level of liquidity within the organization, and the level of organizational debt. Understanding these kinds of issues helps not only to determine the level of investment needed to support digital thrust, but also to determine the digital activities to use to generate new sources of revenue and ways to cut costs.

The *digital component* is that segment of the internal level of an organization's digital environment that houses factors related to the digital condition of the organization. Issues here include, but are not limited to, digital equipment, company Web site strategy, and Web site reliability. Understanding such issues will give management a feel for the levels of digital activities possible in the organization. In essence, this information gives management a sense of the limits on new digital directions that might be implemented.

The *marketing component* is that segment of the internal level of an organization's digital environment containing factors relating to selling goods and services to customers. In this component, factors like the product distribution system, the target market, and the product promotion strategy are studied in detail. Information about this environmental component helps managers to develop ideas for facilitating the marketing process through digital direction.

The *human resource component* is that segment of the internal level of an organization's digital environment that deals with factors related to managing human resources within the organization. Issues like recruiting practices, training programs, and performance appraisal systems are studied in detail. Information about this component serves as a basis for better ensuring that the organization will have appropriate human resources available as needed.

To evaluate the worth of using the Internet to support human resource activities, consider the use of the Internet to attract new employees. Management must recognize that online recruiting has become acceptable or even preferred for finding a new job. Many people go online primarily to surf for job opportunities. In fact, many Internet users admit that their number one reason for going online is to search for a new job. Initially, online recruiting only attracted technology-oriented job seekers. Today, however, the proliferation of home computers has opened the Internet to a diverse array of job postings and job seekers.

Overall, the internal level of the organization's digital environment contains all the resources of the organization and all the actions taken to turn those resources into sold products and services, delivered into the hands of customers. By systematically examining internal components like operations and marketing, management can better appreciate how each component can provide new ideas for an organization's digital direction. In essence, analyzing the internal level will give management ideas for establishing the digital direction that can improve the effectiveness of internal activities.

Summing It Up

In summary, the above model of the digital environment assumes three levels: general, operating, and internal. Each of the three levels contains factors that usually change at different rates and thereby impact digital dimensioning in different amounts of time. Factors in the general environment are more prone to change in the longer run and to thereby impact digital dimensioning in the more distant future. Factors in the operating environment are more prone to change in the more immediate run and thereby to impact digital dimensioning in the "intermediate" future. Factors in the internal environment are more prone to change in the near future and to thereby impact digital dimensioning almost immediately.

Managers must evaluate this generic model of the digital environment and then establish their own digital environments. In many cases, managers will probably establish digital environments that are identical to this generic model. In some cases, however, because issues can impact digital activities within different amounts of time in different organizations, managers may determine that they need to shift environmental factors from one level to another or even establish new factors within levels. Certainly, individual managers are in the best position to build the most accurate model of the digital environment for their organizations. Most importantly, however, a manager should establish a digital environment model to foster common understanding and focused communication about the digital environment throughout the organization.

Who Gathers Information about the Digital Environment?

Once managers have built the overall structures of their unique digital environments, they are ready to start gathering descriptive information about factors in that environment. The levels of their digital environments and the components in each level determine the topics to be studied and the information that will be gathered.

No single method for gathering the information is universally best. The method used must suit the individual circumstances facing the organization. In some organizations, the CEO might want to personally gather the information in order to have a thorough knowledge of the digital environment. In other organizations, a special cross-functional team might be established to gather the information in order to simultaneously build commitment to the accuracy of the information. In still other organizations, a "special" individual could be appointed to do the job in order to make sure that someone is completely accountable for generating useful information. Management should adopt that method that will likely provide the most useful information in describing the digital environment and ultimately the best insights for establishing the organization's digital thrust.

When to Gather Information about the Digital Environment

Many different schedules can be established to scan the digital environments for information. No one schedule is inherently better than any other. Naturally, the schedule most suited to the unique needs of an organization is the one the organization should adopt.

For example, organizations can scan their digital environments continuously. With the continuous schedule, the components of the various levels of the digital environment are monitored constantly. Normally, individuals whose sole responsibility is to provide information about the digital environment to the appropriate organization members operate continuous scanning systems. In other words, for people who operate continuous scanning systems, scanning the digital environment is a full-time endeavor. Organizations with digital environments that are composed of factors that are prone to quick, fast, and seemingly endless change are prime candidates for using a continuous scanning schedule.

Another example is provided by organizations that scan their digital environments on a regular basis. Organizations that adopt regular schedules gather information about the digital environment at selected, regular intervals—perhaps every 6 months or once each year. Certainly, the speed at which digital issues change and develop in an organization should influence the interval length. Such regular schedules establish a routine for measuring digital environment components. Individuals who operate regular scanning systems may not do this scanning full time and may have organizational responsibilities in addition to environmental scanning. Regular scanning systems are probably best suited for organizations with digital environments made up of components that tend to change, but not rapidly enough to necessitate a continuous scanning schedule.

As a third example, organizations can scan their digital environments irregularly. Irregular schedules require the gathering of information only as management sees the need. People operating irregular scanning most likely have other organizational responsibilities also. These people are probably on some type of scanning committee that will be disbanded once the ordered environmental scan is complete. Irregular scanning systems are probably best suited for organizations with digital environments composed of stable components that change very slowly over time.

Interestingly, organizations can adopt some combination of the above schedules as their scanning schedules. As usual, any hybrid schedule should reflect the needs of the organization. Some organizations may determine that some components of their digital environment need to be scanned continuously, other components need to be scanned regularly, and still other components need to be scanned only irregularly. The decision about which scanning schedule to implement should be guided by one important consideration. The organization should choose the scanning schedule that will best provide management with timely information with which to establish appropriate digital direction.

Information Sources

Understanding what constitutes an organization's unique digital environment, determining who will gather information about various components of the digital environment, and deciding when the information will be gathered are all prerequisites to actually gathering the information itself. This section discusses where to look for information about digital environment components.

Naturally, managers must know where to look for needed information when performing an analysis of the digital environment. Sources that managers can use for gathering information are indeed varied. For information about the operating and general levels of the digital environment, possible sources include customers, government documents, and professional journals. For information about the internal level of the digital environment, sources include committee reports, the intranet, and surveys of various kinds.

Keep in mind that no list of such sources is exhaustive. Additionally, different organizations might include more and different sources, depending upon their unique digital environments. Remember, information for analyzing the digital environment is actually the foundation upon which an organization's digital direction is established.

SWOT Analysis: Making Sense of Information Gathered

Thus far, this chapter has discussed the structure of an organization's digital environment as well as the gathering of the information needed to analyze it. This section discusses making sense of the information gathered. Such information can be quite unwieldy and extremely difficult to organize and interpret.

Overall, gathering information about the general, operating, and internal digital environmental levels provides the raw material from which to develop a picture of the organization's digital environment. *SWOT analysis* is a technique for transforming this complex body of information into a simple pattern that enhances both an understanding of and a reaction to the digital environment in which an organization exists.

The acronym *SWOT* stands for *strengths, weaknesses, opportunities,* and *threats.* SWOT analysis attempts to assess the strengths and weaknesses inside an organization and the opportunities and threats outside an organization. SWOT can be used to isolate major digital issues facing an organization through careful analysis of each of these four elements. Managers simply categorize the information generated during the digital environmental analysis into internal strengths or weaknesses and external opportunities or threats and then determine digital direction in response to this categorization.

For an illustration of how to use SWOT to prescribe digital activities for an organization, examine Table 4.1. Assume that a manager has gathered information about the digital environment and then used SWOT to categorize the information as shown in the table. According to this SWOT analysis, one reason the organization is strong is because people have above-average productivity. Based upon this strength, a new digital direction could focus on increasing worker productivity even more. For example, a related digital thrust might include improving the organiza-

Table 4.1 Sample SWOT categorization of information generated via an analysis of the digital environment.

Internal Level Information		General and Operating Levels Information	
Strengths	Weaknesses	Opportunities	Threats
People relationships within division are strong	Team meetings are lacking in attendance	Number of customers is increasing	Products have poor reliability reputations
Financial resources are invested wisely	Costs of operations are increasing	Secondary competitor is going out of business	Relationships with suppliers are lacking
Workers display above-average productivity	Employees lack sufficient knowledge of internal systems	Society's acceptance of buying on the Internet is increasing	Skilled managers are in short supply as the labor market is growing

tion's intranet to provide more immediate feedback to managers regarding worker performance. The hope would be that this more immediate feedback would give managers insights, in less time, about how to help workers become even more productive.

SWOT analysis might suggest that the organization is weak because employees lack sufficient knowledge about internal systems. A related digital thrust could be to develop online training to enhance employee knowledge of internal systems. Next, SWOT analysis might indicate that an opportunity exists due to society's increasing acceptance of making purchases on the Internet. A digital thrust here could be to further develop the organization's ecommerce center, allowing consumers more or different online buying options. Lastly, SWOT might indicate that the organization is threatened because relationships with suppliers are lacking. The digital thrust here could be to build more and better digital interfaces with suppliers. One such interface might be building a digital application that would allow the organization to monitor a supplier's inventory of critical materials in order to better manage workflow in the organization.

Based upon the above SWOT analysis possibilities, using SWOT to help set digital direction in an organization seems very simple. But be careful! This apparent simplicity is actually very deceiving. Even the most seemingly simple SWOT task of properly categorizing environmental information as strengths, weaknesses, opportunities, or threats can be difficult. Also, even after proper categorization, actually determining an appropriate digital thrust can be a difficult task. Perhaps determining the relative importance of each environmental thrust implied by SWOT analysis is the most challenging SWOT-related activity. That is, which new digital thrust should be implemented first? Which new thrust has the lowest priority?

Analysis of the Digital Environment: Improvement Is a Must

Managers analyze digital environments for insights about establishing the digital direction that will help organizations achieve goals effectively and efficiently. Inevitably, such analyses of digital environments will have strengths as well as weaknesses or areas for improvement. Perhaps the information gathered wasn't delivered to managers in a timely fashion. Perhaps the information gathered was improperly categorized during the SWOT analysis. Perhaps a particular environmental component like customers wasn't investigated thoroughly enough.

Managers must continually evaluate the analyses of digital environments for the purpose of improving those analyses and thereby helping organizations to better achieve appropriate digital direction. Improving the analysis of a digital environment is a constant process. Management must continually gather feedback regarding the worth of the results of the analysis and make needed improvements where necessary. Feedback should be gathered from all involved in the digital dimensioning process to determine if the analysis results have been accurate and worthwhile. Overall, managers need to generate answers to three practical and important questions about information gathered during the analysis: How much information about important digital environment components is being gathered? How much information regarding these components should be gathered? How important is it to gather this information?

The Survey for Improving Analysis of Digital Environment is a questionnaire that managers can use to determine the answers to these three questions. The questionnaire, which can be administered online or more traditionally, asks selected employees three questions about each major component of the organization's digital environment. For example, four questions from the survey focus on the customer component of the digital environment. Answers to these questions will help a manager to

determine how much information is being generated about customers, if the amount of customer-related information received is sufficient, and how important that information is for establishing digital direction. The survey also provides respondents the opportunity to give managers ideas about new customer-related information that could be generated during future digital environmental analyses. The entire survey is contained in Appendix A and is available online at www.digitaldimensioning.com. Managers can explore this online completion exercise to acquire a richer understanding of the survey as well as insights about how the survey might be of assistance in their own organizations.

Back to GE

The purpose of this section is to illustrate how the principles of analyzing the digital environment apply to real organizations. Consider the following information as digital dimensioning advice that an ebusiness consultant might give to the top managers of GE's refrigerator manufacturing unit as input for initiating an online presence. To gain maximum benefit from this section, explore GE.com before reading further.

"As top management of the business unit at GE that manufactures refrigerators, you must understand that your segment of GE exists within its own unique digital environment. Your digital environment consists of all the factors both inside and outside your organizational unit that can impact digital activities. These factors include issues like the demographics of employees, operations of suppliers, company marketing efforts, and pending as well as existing digitally related laws.

"In some ways, your digital environment is like the digital environments of other business units at GE. In other ways, however, your digital environment is unique and like that of no other GE business unit. As top management of a GE business unit, you must strive to develop a thorough understanding of your unique digital environment. Only through such an understanding can you determine the direction that your digital efforts should take, and can you consistently pursue related action that will significantly enhance the success of GE's companywide digital activities in the long run.

"You cannot hope to acquire a good understanding of your digital environment without a solid impression of how the digital environment is structured. Think of your business unit's digital environment as having three levels: general, operating, and internal. Consider factors in the general level as being farthest from your unit since these factors usually take the longest amount of time to change and therefore to impact how digital activities should be changed in reaction to them.

"As an illustration of what the general level might mean to you as management, consider personal disposable income in the United States as an issue within the economic component of the general level of your digital environment. As disposable income falls, there will be fewer customers buying products like new refrigerators, and perhaps GE's digital efforts should be stepped up to help retail partners to compete more effectively in this falling-demand situation. Recognize that significant changes in disposable income will probably take years to develop, however, and therefore it will be years before you need to make a change in your digital direction. You must consistently monitor issues like disposable income, however, to know when they change enough to warrant changing your digital direction. Overall, choose those factors that exist in the general level of your unique digital environment, monitor them appropriately, and change your digital direction per changes in those factors.

"Think of the operating level of your digital environment as being closer to the organization than the general level. Accordingly, think of factors in this level as usually changing more quickly and having the potential of impacting your digital direction more quickly than factors in the general level. This level includes factors like your customers, your competition, and your suppliers.

"As an example of what changes in the operating level might mean to you as management, consider this scenario about the Whirlpool Corporation. Assume that Whirlpool, a formidable competitor, begins digitally enhancing its retail partners' ability to feature new refrigerator models as well as old models not presently in stores but that can be ordered with fast delivery. Whirlpool's action should probably be thought of as a change in your operating environment that should impact your digital direction. After all, if you do not react to Whirlpool's digital thrust, your market share could be significantly eroded in a relatively short time.

"Overall, choose the factors that constitute your operating environment, monitor them, and change your digital direction in accordance with changes in these factors. Since factors in the operating level tend to change more quickly than factors in the general level, you may want to monitor operating-level factors more often than general-level factors.

"Think of the internal level of your business unit's digital environment as being closer to the organization than either the general or operating level. As such, think of factors in the internal level as perhaps changing more rapidly and impacting the digital direction of the organization more quickly than factors in any other digital environment level. The internal level includes factors like marketing programs, financial performance, and human resources.

"As an example of how changes in the internal level might impact your digital direction, consider the following scenario. Assume that you've just been handed a report indicating that the financial performance of your unit was extremely poor in the last operating period. As one reaction to this poor performance, you may decide to evaluate and reprioritize upcoming expenditures. Certainly, this evaluation and reprioritization could have an immediate impact on digital direction. Overall, choose the factors that constitute the internal level of your digital environment, monitor them, and change digital direction as necessitated by changes in the factors.

"Monitoring your digital environment requires that, from time to time, you gather information describing the components of each level. You may decide to scan different environmental levels at different times and some levels more often than others. Comparing information from one environmental scan with that of another will help determine trends in the factors and, as a result, the modifications of digital direction that may be needed in the future.

"Perhaps your highest challenge in analyzing your digital environment is making sense of the information gathered to describe it. Use SWOT analysis to help you interpret what the descriptive information means. SWOT requires that you categorize each piece of information gathered as organizational strength, weakness, opportunity, or threat. Once you have completed the SWOT profiles, you'll have leads about which direction digital thrust should take.

"Remember that analyzing your digital environment is a constant, iterative process. As such, maintain focus on improving your analysis process. Continually gather feedback from people about how to improve the analysis. Also, you can use the Survey for Improving Analysis of the Digital Environment to determine if you're gathering enough information or if you should gather other information. The survey also helps you to evaluate the usefulness of gathered information for determining digital direction."

Digital Dimensioning Resolutions

- Make sure others in your organization know the meaning of *digital environment*.
- Communicate the purpose of analyzing your digital environment.
- Determine factors to include in the general level of your digital environment.
- Determine factors to include in the operating level of your digital environment.
- Determine factors to include in the internal level of your digital environment.
- Build and circulate a complete model of your digital environment.
- Determine your sources of analysis information.
- Determine how often you need to scan your digital environment.
- Determine who is responsible for actually gathering your information.
- Use SWOT to help interpret information describing the digital environment.
- Constantly improve your process for analyzing the digital environment.

chapter 5

Establishing Digital Direction

Executive Preview

This chapter discusses the principles that managers should follow to establish digital direction in organizations. *Digital direction* is defined as an organization's broad digital thrust consistent with the accomplishment of organizational purpose. A manager can formalize digital direction primarily through both a statement of digital direction and digital support goals. The *statement of digital direction* expresses how digital activities in an organization will be focused in order to help accomplish organizational purpose. *Digital support goals* are targets that, when reached, will aid the attainment of established organizational goals and thereby help fulfill organizational purpose. Additionally, the chapter discusses the *digital support grid*, a practical management tool for assessing the impact of activities aimed at reaching an organization's digital support goals. The opening discussion focuses on General Motors, and the concluding discussion offers digital dimensioning advice that a consultant could have given General Motors management as input for initiating its digital presence. The chapter ends with resolutions that you can make to enhance the ebusiness competitiveness of *your* organization.

Spotlight

General Motors Establishes Digital Direction[1]

General Motors Corporation (GM) is a world-class designer, manufacturer, and marketer of cars and trucks. Popular brand names include Chevrolet, Pontiac, GMC, Oldsmobile, Buick, Cadillac, and Saturn. The company has more than 150 locations operating in over 30 states and 100 cities in the United States. These locations are primarily engaged in the final assembly of GM cars and trucks as well as the warehousing and distribution of repair parts for present and past car and truck models. The company has similar locations in Canada and over 50 other countries including Germany, the United Kingdom, and Brazil. GM employs more than 350,000 people.

In the past, GM has been described as a technological backwater, and for good reason. For instance, the time it took to develop a new car stretched to nearly 4 years, engineers in the United States were unable to communicate with engineers abroad, and marketing information was difficult to access. Like the rest of the U.S. auto industry, it took GM years to adopt even straightforward technological developments like the air bag.

Recently, however, GM management initiated a new ebusiness thrust for the company. The company even created a new operating unit to coordinate and manage the global proliferation of this new thrust. Part of the purpose for the new thrust was to use the Internet to connect with car buyers in a new, exciting fashion that would lead to better relationships with customers. Based upon this action taken at GM, management obviously believes that customers are ready for Web-initiated car buying.

Certainly, building powerful relationships with customers via the Internet can be invaluable to GM. However, the scope of GM's digital direction, while certainly including customer emphasis, will also be broad enough to reap the benefits of Internet relationships with many other GM stakeholders like suppliers, the communities in which GM operates, and employees.

Organizational benefits derived from GM's new Internet thrust will likely be broad and varied. In fact, some managers maintain that this new Internet thrust could be the beginning of the reinvention of the General Motors Corporation.

Principles for Establishing Digital Direction

What's Ahead? The Spotlight discussed management's recently initiated focus on Internet-related activities at General Motors Corporation. Commendably, one component focuses on developing relationships with customers. Management's logic is that such relationships will ultimately contribute to vehicle sales and thereby enhance company success. This logic seems impeccable. To gain maximum benefit from the Internet, the management of any organization should establish digital direction that is broad enough to include relationships with all organizational stakeholders. The real challenge facing managers like those at GM is not simply to establish sound customer relationships via the Internet, but to establish digital direction that is appropriate for the overall organization. This chapter is a detailed discussion of step 3 of the digital dimensioning process, establishing digital direction.

Enlisting digital expertise, the subject of Chapter 3, is the first step of the digital dimensioning process. After digital expertise has been enlisted, the digital dimensioning process continues, with management using this expertise to analyze the organization's digital environment, the subject of Chapter 4. Armed with information discovered during this analysis, management takes the next step of the digital dimensioning process, establishing the organization's digital direction. Overall, this chapter defines digital direction and presents the statement of digital direction and digital support goals as the means for building digital direction in organizations.

What Is Digital Direction?

Digital direction is defined as an organization's broad digital thrust consistent with the accomplishment of organizational purpose. As implied by this definition, digital direction has no true meaning apart from organizational purpose. Without a thorough understanding of organizational purpose, developing a useful digital direction relies more on chance than on management expertise. The content and philosophy of an organization's digital direction should reflect the true nature of organizational purpose. In fact, establishing digital direction is simply a tool for enhancing the accomplishment of organizational purpose. Although establishing digital direction is not management's only means for accomplishing organizational purpose, given our modern global business arena, it's certainly a very valuable one.

Tools for Establishing Digital Direction

Managers have two main tools for establishing digital direction in organizations. These tools are a statement of digital direction and digital support goals. The following sections describe each of these tools in detail.

Statement of Digital Direction

A *statement of digital direction* is a short, broadly stated proclamation of the organization's digital thrust. A statement of digital direction outlines how an organization's broad digital direction will contribute to the accomplishment of organizational purpose or mission statement. Preferably, the statement of digital direction is in written form and has been adopted within the organization as a guideline for future decision making as well as a tool for building the organization's digital culture. The statement of digital direction should be consistent with information uncovered during the analysis of an organization's digital environment.

Information for developing the statement of digital direction can come from many different exhibits that establish courses of broad organizational direction. At Johnson & Johnson, for example, management uses "Our Credo" to establish broad organizational direction. The company manufactures and sells a wide range of health care products throughout the world. Essentially, "Our Credo" outlines how the company approaches relationships with stakeholders like doctors and nurses, employees, and stockholders. "Our Credo" also describes the company orientation toward research and innovation and appears on the company Web site.

At Merck & Company, management establishes broad organizational direction through a company exhibit called "Mission Statement." Merck is a world-renowned, global pharmaceutical company. "Mission Statement" outlines the overall purpose of the company and the values that drive the company. The values highlighted relate to human life, ethics, and scientific excellence. Merck's "Mission Statement" is on the company Web site and appears in Figure 5.1.

Figure 5.1   Merck's Mission Statement describes the company, its mission, and critical company values.

Merck & Co., Inc. is a leading research-driven pharmaceutical products and services company. Merck discovers, develops, manufactures and markets a broad range of innovative products to improve human and animal health. The Merck-Medco Managed Care Division manages pharmacy benefits for more than 40 million Americans, encouraging the appropriate use of medicines and providing disease management programs.

OUR MISSION

The mission of Merck is to provide society with superior products and services—innovations and solutions that improve the quality of life and satisfy customer needs—to provide employees with meaningful work and advancement opportunities and investors with a superior rate of return.

OUR VALUES

1. **Our business is preserving and improving human life.** All of our actions must be measured by our success in achieving this goal. We value above all our ability to serve everyone who can benefit from the appropriate use of our products and services, thereby providing lasting consumer satisfaction.

2. **We are committed to the highest standards of ethics and integrity.** We are responsible to our customers, to Merck employees and their families, to the environments we inhabit, and to the societies we serve worldwide. In discharging our responsibilities, we do not take professional or ethical shortcuts. Our interactions with all segments of society must reflect the high standards we profess.

3. **We are dedicated to the highest level of scientific excellence and commit our research to improving human and animal health and the quality of life.** We strive to identify the most critical needs of consumers and customers, we devote our resources to meeting those needs.

4. **We expect profits, but only from work that satisfies customer needs and benefits humanity.** Our ability to meet our responsibilities depends on maintaining a financial position that invites investment in leading-edge research and that makes possible effective delivery of research results.

5. **We recognize that the ability to excel—to most competitively meet society's and customers' needs—depends on the integrity, knowledge, imagination, skill, diversity and teamwork of employees, and we value these qualities most highly.** To this end, we strive to create an environment of mutual respect, encouragement and teamwork—a working environment that rewards commitment and performance and is responsive to the needs of employees and their families.

At McDonald's Corporation, broad organizational direction is established through a statement of vision. Company vision emphasizes being the world's best quick-service restaurant experience for customers and providing outstanding quality, service, and cleanliness. The vision statement also highlights employee relations and a focus on profitability. "McDonald's Vision" appears on the company Web site and proclaims that the company will be the best employer of people in all communities served.

As a last example of an organization exhibit that establishes broad organizational direction, consider "Baxter's Values" at Baxter International. Baxter International is a global leader in delivering critical therapies for life-threatening conditions. Baxter technologies relate primarily to human blood and circulatory system problems. "Baxter's Values" contains company ideals for building respect, responding to challenges, and obtaining expected results from operations. "Baxter's Values" can also be found at the company's Web site.

Differentiating definitionally among exhibits like mission statement, values statements, and company credos is not critically important here. What is important, however, is to recognize that many organizations have established statements that describe broad organizational direction. Management must recognize that such statements can provide invaluable insight about how the digital direction of an organization should be established.

Statement of Digital Direction: The Foundation

Naturally, specific information contained in a statement of digital direction will vary from organization to organization. Regardless of specific content, however, statements of digital direction must reflect an overall understanding of the features and characteristics of an organization. In essence, this understanding is the foundation upon which a useful statement of digital direction is built. This foundation includes:

- *Understanding the organization's products or services.* This understanding reflects thorough knowledge of what a company offers its customers.

- *Understanding the organization's customers.* This understanding shows a knowledge of the markets and customers that the organization serves. Knowing who these customers are and where they are located is of immense help in crafting the best statement of digital direction for an organization.

- ***Understanding how the organization employs digital and other technology.*** This understanding focuses on a knowledge of, for example, the techniques and processes the organization uses to produce goods and services. This understanding may also consist of knowledge of established digital techniques used by an organization.

- ***Understanding the organization's goal areas.*** This understanding reflects a knowledge of the established realms in which established targets of the organization exist. These realms typically represent various facets of dealings with key stakeholders, such as shareholders, customers, employees, suppliers, government, and the community in which the organization exists.

- ***Understanding the organization's core values.*** This understanding shows a knowledge of the company values that drive significant organizational activities of all kinds. Statements of digital direction must be consistent with an organization's core values.

- ***Understanding the organization's self-concept.*** This understanding is knowledge about what an organization thinks of itself. For example, an organization might see itself primarily as socially responsible, or as a low-cost producer, or as a leader in a particular industry. A statement of digital direction should reinforce an organization's perception of self.

- ***Understanding the organization's desired public image.*** This understanding pertains to knowledge about how the organization would like the public to view it. Perhaps an organization would like the public to view it primarily as promoting diversity, as being progressive in handling employees, or as having high-quality products. A statement of digital direction should enhance the establishment of the organization's desired public image.

Sample Statement of Digital Direction

Specific procedures for crafting a statement of digital direction would be useless. Unlike developing organizational financial statements, which should be accomplished by following specific rules, developing content for a statement of digital direction should be left mostly to management judgment.

Although the exact form of a statement of digital direction is primarily inconsequential, its function in each organization should be identical. The function of a statement of digital direction is to give broad direction to organization members about how to employ digital thrust to help accomplish organizational purpose. In essence, the statement of digital direction gives all organization members broad direction for making decisions about the types of digital activities to employ, guidance about the extent of digital activity to employ, and an overall orientation about how digital thrust fits into organizational philosophy.

A sample statement of digital direction for a fictitious supermarket called Buy Here Now, Inc., is presented in Figure 5.2. This sample statement has many interesting features. First, the statement makes it clear to all organization members that Buy Here Now management places high value on using digital activities to accomplish organizational purpose. The statement also establishes a consistency between the company's overall orientation toward the use of technology and its support of digital activities. In other words, employing digital activities at Buy Here Now is simply consistent with established organizational tradition and in no way should be seen as controversial. In addition, the sample statement establishes the organization's digital thrust as a vehicle for gaining significant competitive advantage through improved digital relationships with all stakeholders. Perhaps the most interesting information

Figure 5.2   A sample statement of digital directions for a fictitious supermarket chain.

STATEMENT OF DIGITAL DIRECTION
Buy Here Now, Inc.

Buy Here Now, Inc., recognizes the great importance of employing digital activities in accomplishing organizational purpose. Our national supermarket chain is progressive, growth-oriented, and always at the leading edge of technology. One new exciting opportunity that we now have is employing digital technology in building significant competitive advantage over other supermarkets. We will vigorously employ digital applications in our relationships with all major stakeholders. Our search for new ways to build relationships with customers, suppliers, employees, and the communities we serve will be tireless. Every person in our company shares the responsibility of discovering and participating in implementing new digital applications in any area that will help *Buy Here Now, Inc.,* to be more successful.

conveyed in this sample statement is management's attitude that everyone at Buy Here Now should be thinking about how to improve the company's digital presence.

In sum, many organizations have adopted formal statements that describe the organization's broad direction. Names for such statements include mission statements, codes of conduct, vision statements, and statements of corporate values. Managers should craft statements of digital direction to support established organizational direction. In some cases, management may be able to adequately establish an organization's digital direction simply by adding carefully crafted statements to documents like a mission statement or a vision statement. In other cases, where no established documents for organizational direction exist, statements of digital direction should perhaps be more detailed, covering topics like earnings, innovation, or productivity. In this situation, knowledge for crafting the statement can be generated through interviews with various organization members, company surveys, and observation of organizational operations.

Digital Support Goals

In addition to a statement of digital direction, managers should use digital support goals to establish digital direction. *Digital support goals* are targets that, when reached, will aid in the attainment of established organizational goals and thereby help fulfill organizational purpose. In essence, management studies organizational goals and develops digital support to enhance the achievement of those goals.

As an example of how a digital support goal might be developed, consider circumstances at McDonald's Corporation, a company whose vision statement was discussed earlier in this chapter. McDonald's is composed of a worldwide chain of restaurants offering a substantially uniform fast-food menu consisting of items such as hamburgers, cheeseburgers, chicken sandwiches, and french fries.

McDonald's has an established goal of giving back to the communities it serves. As one example of how this giving back occurs at McDonald's, consider the Ronald McDonald Care Mobile, a program started to provide better health care access to disadvantaged children in communities across the United States. Working with local hospitals and health systems, the Ronald McDonald Care Mobile brings medical and dental services directly into neighborhoods with unmet health care needs.

Management at McDonald's can enhance the attainment of its established goal of giving back to the community by establishing related digital support goals. For example, management might establish the digital support goal of allowing visitors to its corporate Web site to make contributions to the Ronald McDonald Care Mobile project. In addition, a digital support goal of allowing patients to make appointments online might enhance operations efficiency. As another example, a digital support goal might include establishing wireless intranet communication between the care mobile staff and hospitals. In essence, the stream of digital support goals that might enhance McDonald's goal of giving back to the community via the care mobile seems endless. Of course, digital support goals will not be management's only means of giving back through mobile health care. These digital support goals could, however, be a very valuable enhancement to the success of the mobile health care program.

Areas for Digital Support Goals

Most management theorists and practicing managers agree that, in order to properly guide an organization, management should establish an array of goals that focus on a number of different, important operational areas. Naturally, in establishing an organization's digital direction, management should establish a corresponding array of digital support goals aimed at enhancing the accomplishment of these operational goals. The following are several areas in which organizational goals are commonly set and in which management should expect to set corresponding digital support goals:

Earnings   Management typically sets profit goals for organizations. The *profit goal* stipulates how much excess of revenue over cost that management would like to retain. In reaching a profit goal, management must outline the means for accomplishing the goal and then pursue the means. In maintaining an organization's digital dimension, management should also outline digital support goals that will enhance the accomplishment of profit goals. For example, assume that an organization sets the goal of increasing profit by 10 percent in a year. A related digital support goal could be to inform salespeople, via a new intranet connection, of real-time inventory levels. Such information would be aimed at helping salespeople to sell more products by more accurately meeting customer delivery needs. As this new revenue increased over the cost of the intranet connection, a contribution to increased profit goal would be established. In essence, the digital support goal has enhanced the accomplishment of the organizational goal.

Innovation   Management also commonly sets innovation goals for organizations. The *innovation goal* outlines management's commitment to finding new, better methods of conducting organizational business. Innovation goals outline management's posture toward finding new and better operational methods. As an example of an innovation goal, assume that management establishes the target of improving communication with customers. Naturally, many different kinds of activity, digital as well as nondigital, could be aimed at reaching this improvement target. One digital support goal for improving communication could be to establish an email communication program that informs customers about new products the company is developing.

New York Life Insurance Company provides a good example of digital innovation. One of the nation's top five providers of life insurance policies, annuities, and mutual funds, this company has an established goal of providing more innovative customer service, and the company recently established a related digital support goal. The digital support goal involved planning and launching the Virtual Service Center, an online vehicle for allowing customers to request policy cash as well as loan and dividend quotes. The Virtual Service Center also allows customers to submit requests to change premium payment schedules or pay premiums by using loans or dividends. The Virtual Service Center is a significant digital accomplishment supporting an established goal of better customer service and is already yielding great benefits to the company. These benefits should only increase as the company learns more about how to best use the center.[2]

Productivity   *Productivity* refers to the level of an organization's output in relation to the resources needed to produce the output. The fewer resources needed to produce output, the more productive the organization. *Productivity goals* refer to the level of productivity that an organization is striving to reach.

Recently, Freddie Mac, one of the country's biggest mortgage underwriters, set the organizational goal of increasing productivity in generating home loans. As a digital support goal for enhancing this productivity goal, the organization set the goal of launching Loan Prospector, an Internet-based system that automatically and quickly underwrites a home loan. For Freddie Mac the productivity benefits have been enormous. Loan transaction volume has increased 200 percent in a year without adding any more staff.[3]

Social Responsibility   *Social responsibility* is the obligation of business to help improve the welfare of society while it strives to reach other organizational goals. *Social responsibility goals* are organizational targets that, when achieved, will not only contribute to the success of the organization, but contribute to the general welfare of society. Only a few decades ago, setting social responsibility goals in organizations was quite controversial. Today, however, setting these goals is commonplace and considered instrumental in gaining organizational success.

Digital support goals in many organizations focus on using the company Web site to organize social responsibility activities. Take International Business Machines Corporation as an example. IBM is known worldwide for providing customers with information technology solutions in areas like systems, software, and services.

Over the last 10 years, IBM has earned one of the most notable records in the area of social responsibility. The company regularly contributes gifts such as cash, equipment, and the services of its employees to nonprofit organizations and educational institutions throughout the world. IBM's stated social responsibility goal is to help people use information technology to improve the quality of life for themselves and others.

IBM uses its corporate Web site as a focal point for organizing its social responsibility activities. At the site, IBM keeps stakeholders informed about company social responsibility activities in an area it calls community relations. In the community relations section, IBM tells stakeholders about the company's social responsibility efforts and how to participate in those efforts. In essence, the Web site is used as an important vehicle supporting the accomplishment of IBM's social responsibility goals.

Managers should use established organizational goals as guides for the types of digital support goals to establish. The above discussion illustrates how digital support goals can be developed to help accomplish an organization's earnings, productivity, innovation, and social responsibility goals. These established goals, however, are for example purposes only and are not meant to be an exhaustive list of organizational goals. Organizational goals are commonly set in many other areas like market standing, communication, and human resource management. Managers must keep in mind that goals established from organization to organization can and should vary, depending upon unique organizational circumstances. Correspondingly, managers also must keep in mind that digital support goals can and should vary from organization to organization, depending upon an organization's established goal set.

High-Quality Digital Support Goals

Although many organizations have digital support goals, some goals are more useful than others. The quality of digital support goals largely determines their usefulness. Guidelines can be followed to help managers develop high-quality and therefore more useful digital support goals. Several such guidelines are:

• *Establish digital support goals that are specific.* Specific digital support goals indicate exactly what should be accomplished, who should accomplish it, and within what time frame they should accomplish it. Specific details eliminate confusion about what digital support goals require from organization members. Furthermore, more specific digital support goals make it easier for management to accomplish the step in the digital dimensioning process that follows setting digital direction, developing digital strategies. Specific, high-quality digital support goals provide a solid foundation on which managers can construct appropriate digital strategies.

• *Establish digital support goals that require an appropriate level of effort.* Digital support goals should be set high enough that employees must somewhat extend themselves to achieve them. Digital support goals that challenge employees' abilities are generally more interesting and more motivating for organization members than easily attained digital support goals. Managers should keep in mind, however, that if workers view the goals as too difficult or impossible to reach, they may informally and independently decide not to waste valuable time and effort in attempting to reach them.

• *Establish digital support goals that are flexible.* Managers must continually monitor established organizational goals and the digital environment to recognize when digital support goals should be modified. Managers should caution organization members to expect such change in digital support goals so that the change is anticipated and acted upon as soon and as conscientiously as possible.

- *Establish digital support goals that are measurable.* A measurable digital support goal, sometimes called an *operational digital support goal,* is a digital support goal stated in such a way that an attempt to attain it can be measured and compared with the goal itself to determine whether it actually has been attained. Confusion about whether digital goals have been attained can result in conflict, poor relations between managers and workers, and ultimately failure to reach the goals.

- *Establish digital support goals to be consistent with organizational objectives for both the long run and short run.* Most organizations have established long-term organizational goals that stipulate organizational targets to be hit within a 3- to 5-year period. Most organizations also have established short-run goals that are consistent with established long-term goals and stipulate organizational targets to be reached within 1 or 2 years. As a general rule, these shorter-run goals are derived from and lead to the attainment of established longer-run goals. Managers should establish digital support goals to enhance the accomplishment of both the short- and long-run goals of an organization.

Digital Support Grid

The *digital support grid* is a matrix that uses both effectiveness and efficiency in determining the overall character of an organization's digital support activities. The digital support grid appears in Figure 5.3 and, as you can see, is divided into four quadrants representing four primary profiles of digital support activity. Each of these profiles is symbolized by a particular type of car (jalopy, roadster, car with an oil problem, and car with a steering problem) to give managers a quick, easy way for thinking about, categorizing, and improving digital activities.

Digital support effectiveness is the degree to which digital efforts actually help an organization to reach its digital support goals. The more digital activity helps to reach the goals, the more effective the action is said to be. As illustrated in Figure 5.3, the effectiveness of digital action taken within organizations can be viewed as existing on a continuum ranging from very effective to very ineffective.

Digital support efficiency is the proportion of resources allocated to performing digital activities that finally contributes to reaching digital

Figure 5.3 Digital support grid.

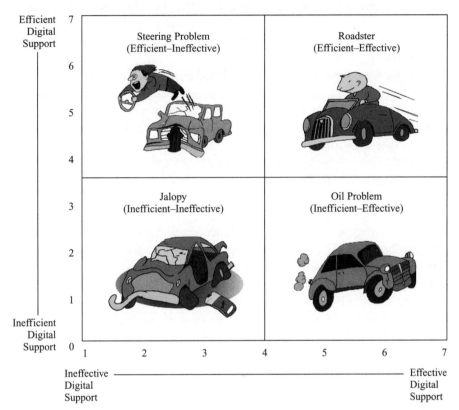

support goals. Digital support efficiency focuses on the best use of important organizational resources like people, materials, equipment, money, and time.

Essentially, digital support efficiency focuses on waste. The higher the proportion of resources used to contribute to the attainment of a digital support goal, the more efficient and less wasteful the digital support activity is said to be. The lower the proportion of resources, the more inefficient and more wasteful the digital support activity. As with the effectiveness of digital action, Figure 5.3 illustrates that the efficiency of digital action can be thought of as being on a continuum ranging from inefficient to efficient. Inefficient means that a significant proportion of organizational resources are being wasted as digital support activities are carried out.

The digital support grid contains a virtually limitless number of efficiency-effectiveness combinations for describing the status of an organization's digital support activities. For simplicity and clarity, the grid is divided into four quadrants. Each quadrant and its related car symbol are discussed below:

Inefficient-Effective: The Oil Problem   The bottom right-hand quadrant of the digital support grid represents digital support activities that are inefficient but effective. This quadrant represents digital activities that enhance the attainment of digital support goals, but waste significant organizational resources in the process. A car with an oil problem symbolizes these activities. The car can transport passengers to a goal destination, but the trip is more costly than necessary because of wasted oil.

Inefficient-Ineffective: The Jalopy   The bottom left-hand quadrant of the digital support grid characterizes digital support activities that are both inefficient and ineffective. This quadrant represents digital activities that not only do not significantly enhance the attainment of digital support goals, but waste organizational resources in the process. A jalopy car symbolizes these activities. This car has difficulty arriving at a goal destination and wastes resources as it operates.

Efficient-Ineffective: The Steering Problem   The upper left-hand quadrant of the digital support grid characterizes digital support activities that are efficient but ineffective. This quadrant represents digital activities that do not significantly enhance the attainment of digital support goals although they do not waste organizational resources in the process. A car with a steerling problem symbolizes these activities. Even though this car does not waste resources as it operates, it has difficulty arriving at a goal destination because it often veers off in the wrong direction.

Efficient-Effective: Roadster   The upper right-hand quadrant of the digital support grid characterizes digital support activities that are both efficient and effective. This quadrant represents digital activities that significantly enhance the attainment of digital support goals and do not waste organizational resources. A roadster symbolizes these activities. This car arrives at a goal destination and does so without wasting oil or gas. The roadster is typically fun to drive and arrives at destinations quickly.

Summing Up   Overall, the digital support grid helps managers to categorize their digital support activities on the basis of effectiveness and efficiency. Once this categorization is complete, managers can take action to improve digital activities when necessary. Appendix B contains the Survey for Improving Digital Support and can provide managers with information about how to make their digital support activities both effective and efficient. In other words, management should aspire to turn cars with oil problems, jalopies, and cars with steering problems into roadsters.

Back to General Motors

This section of the chapter illustrates how digital dimensioning principles apply to real organizations. Consider the following information as digital dimensioning advice that an ebusiness consultant might have given General Motors management as input for initiating its digital presence. To gain maximum benefit from this section, explore gm.com before reading further.

"As management at General Motors you must establish a digital direction for your company. Your digital direction is a broad digital thrust that is consistent with accomplishing GM's purpose. Remember, your digital thrust has no meaning apart from your organizational purpose. Think of digital thrust as a tool for helping you to fulfill GM's purpose. GM's digital thrust must be based upon and be consistent with GM's purpose.

"You can use two primary tools to establish your digital direction here at GM. The first tool is a statement of digital direction. Your statement of digital direction should be a relatively short proclamation outlining the broad, overall thrust of GM's digital activities. You can write the statement yourself or involve others in its framing. Involving others might help you to build organizational awareness and commitment to the digital direction.

"Whoever writes your statement of digital direction should make sure that it reflects established GM documents that outline the organization's established direction. Such reflection is critical. Any established documents describing issues like GM's business philosophy, mission, business values, or management's vision for GM will be very valuable in helping you to conceptualize the fundamental tenets driving GM. This conceptualization should be the driving force in writing your statement of digital direction.

"Remember, there is no exact blueprint for framing your statement of digital direction. In fact, you may find that simply adding a few words to the GM mission statement will suffice as your statement. On the other hand, you may want to craft an independent, stand alone statement. An independent statement of digital direction should refer to, or be based upon an understanding of, GM's products or services, GM's target market, the areas upon which GM's goals focus, GM's core values, GM's self-concept, and GM's targeted public image.

"Use digital support goals as your second major tool for establishing digital direction at GM. Digital support goals are targets that, when attained, will contribute to reaching established GM goals. For example, an Internet-related goal of building better relationships with customers can be considered a digital support goal aimed at enhancing GM's already established goal of building customer relationships.

"Establish digital support goals for as many of GM's established goals as possible. Be creative in developing digital support goals related to established goals in areas like earnings, innovation, productivity, social responsibility, communication, training and development, and product quality. In establishing your digital support goals, make sure they are specific in outlining action to be taken, require an appropriate level of effort to achieve, are flexible in that they can be changed as circumstances change, are measurable to establish that indeed they have been reached, and are consistent with both long- and short-run goals at GM.

"Evaluate your digital support goals for both efficiency and effectiveness. You should evaluate digital support goals as you are developing them. You should also evaluate digital support goals as people are striving to reach them at GM. In terms of effectiveness, make sure that digital support goals are aimed at appropriate targets and that people are indeed reaching those targets. In terms of efficiency, make sure that people are not wasting resources while pursuing digital support goals. In essence, get rid of your jalopy, fix your oil leaks, fix your steering mechanism, and drive a digital roadster."

Digital Dimensioning Resolutions

- Make sure that everyone in your organization understands the meaning of *digital direction*.
- Establish a statement of digital direction for your organization.
- Make your statement of digital direction consistent with organizational purpose.
- Craft your statement of digital direction to reflect established statements of organizational direction like mission and vision statements.
- Base your statement of digital direction upon an acute awareness of issues like your products and services, your target market, and your use of technology.
- Establish digital support goals to help reach established organizational goals.
- Following the pattern of commonly established goals in organizations, establish digital support goals in areas like earnings, innovation, productivity, and social responsibility.
- Make your digital support goals specific, challenging enough, and flexible.
- Make your digital support goals flexible, measurable, and consistent with established organizational goals for both the short and long run.
- Plan activities to reach digital support goals to be efficient.
- Review activities aimed at achieving digital support goals to ensure efficiency.
- Plan activities to reach digital support goals to be effective.
- Review activities aimed at reaching digital support goals to ensure effectiveness.
- Per the digital support grid, fix your oil leaks.
- Per the digital support grid, fix your steering mechanism.
- Per the digital support grid, junk your jalopy.
- Per the digital support grid, drive a roadster.

chapter 6

Formulating
Digital Strategy

Executive Preview

This chapter presents insights that managers should follow to
formulate digital strategy in organizations. *Digital strategy* is
defined as an organization's master plan outlining how digital
activities will support the organization's statement of digital
direction, digital support goals, and, ultimately, organizational success. In formulating digital strategy, the chapter recommends that
managers consider organizational functions, business operations,
corporate operations, and digital tactics. Managers are also given
insights about how to add value to an organization through digital strategy. The opening discussion focuses on American Airlines
and ends with digital dimensioning advice that an ebusiness consultant could have given American Airlines management as input
for initiating digital activities. The chapter concludes with resolutions that you can make to enhance the ebusiness competitiveness of *your* organization.

The Internet Takes Off at American Airlines[1]

American Airlines is one of the largest passenger airlines in the world. American provides scheduled jet service to more than 169 destinations throughout North America, the Caribbean, Latin America, Europe, and the Pacific. In addition, American is also one of the world's largest providers of air freight and mail services.

In terms of digital strategy, American Airlines employs the Internet in many different ways. To develop its digital strategy, American relied heavily upon advice from its department heads. Management felt that since the department heads were closely and continually involved in running their departments on a day-to-day basis, they were in the best position to advise management about how to use the Internet to the best advantage of the company.

Essentially, American's digital strategy supports its wide array of operating activities. Major thrusts of the strategy focus on supporting the company call center, sales management, and employee scheduling. In terms of the call center, digital activities provide support by allowing customers to purchase tickets via the company site in addition to the telephone. In terms of sales management, the company's online presence allows dead inventory or empty seats to be sold at discounted prices. Naturally, this digital activity is very valuable in that it adds incremental dollars to company sales efforts. In terms of employee scheduling, the company's intranet presence allows employees to access employee information like work schedules quickly and easily from anywhere in the world.

Fortunately for the company, American Airlines was quick to formulate and implement its digital strategy. Some of its U.S. competitors like Delta Air Lines and United Air Lines, however, are also making significant digital strides. For now, though, American does seem to hold a significant competitive advantage over some of its foreign competitors. Malaysia Airlines and Thai Airways International, for example, seem to be more in preliminary phases of initiating digital activities that are competitive with those of American. Malaysia Airlines' Web site seems lacking because it is mostly limited to providing customers with flight schedules. Thai Airways requires customers who book tickets through its Web site to physically go to a Thai Airways office to pay for the tickets rather than paying at the Web site.

Most assuredly, American's domestic and foreign competitors are emphasizing the development of digital thrust to build competitive advantage. The message seems clear. To maintain a position of strength in the airlines industry, American Airlines must continuously strive to refine and expand its digital strategy.

Principles for Formulating Digital Strategy

What's Ahead? The Spotlight discussed recent digital thrust at American Airlines. The company has indeed initiated worthwhile digital activities supporting its call center, sales management, and employee scheduling. To maintain a digital competitive advantage over the long run, however, management at American must continually refine and expand its digital strategy. This chapter is a detailed discussion of step 4 of the digital dimensioning process, formulating digital strategy. Managers like those at American Airlines would find valuable insights in this chapter about developing digital strategy for organizations.

Introduction

Step 1 of the digital dimensioning process is enlisting digital expertise. After digital expertise has been enlisted, the digital dimensioning process continues with step 2, using this expertise to analyze the organization's digital environment. Armed with information discovered during this analysis, management takes step 3 of the digital dimensioning process, establishing the organization's digital direction. This chapter focuses on step 4 of the digital dimensioning process, formulating digital strategy. This step ensures that an organization fulfills its statement of digital direction and reaches its digital support goals.

Defining Digital Strategy

Digital strategy is defined as an organization's master plan that outlines how digital activities will lead to the fulfillment of the organization's statement of digital direction and the accomplishment of digital support goals. Since by their very nature the statement of digital direction and the accomplishment of digital support goals contribute to the fulfillment of both organizational purpose and organizational goals, digital strategy ultimately helps to ensure the overall success of the organization.

Formulating Digital Strategy

Formulating digital strategy is the process of actually developing digital strategy. Formulating digital strategy embodies the organization's best efforts to think smart about its digital future. In essence, when formulating digital strategy, management thinks about important factors like those included in Figure 6.1. Related issues could include how to use digital action to position its goods or services against those of competitors, how to forge positive relationships with customers, how to enhance and facilitate the use of core competencies, and how to prepare for shifts in the digital environment. To put it briefly, formulating digital strategy is a no-nonsense management process aimed at building an organization's competitive strength.

Figure 6.1 Managers should carefully consider four important factors when formulating digital strategy.

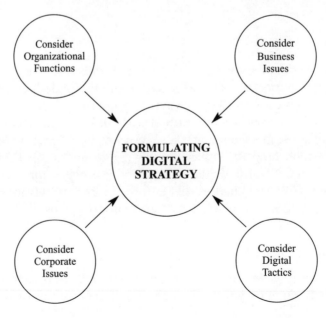

Formulating digital strategy is primarily an analytical effort that relies heavily on judgment and creativity. It draws critical input from the results of the analysis of the digital environment, as discussed in Chapter 4, and focuses on matching the organization to its environment. Overall, digital strategy formulation provides the organization with an integrative plan that details how the organization will fulfill its statement of digital direction. This formulation process further refines the more general notions of earlier steps of the digital dimensioning process regarding how the organization should function in the digital arena.

The four critical organizational factors depicted in Figure 6.1 are (1) organizational functions, (2) business issues, (3) corporate issues, and (4) digital tactics. Each factor and its possible impact on digital strategy are highlighted in the following sections.

Consider Organizational Functions

An *organizational function* is defined as a major activity performed within an organization. Typically, organizational functions involve activities like marketing, human resource management, and operations. Functional emphasis in digital strategy is aimed at supporting the performance of major organizational functions via digital activities. The following sections discuss several major organizational functions and examples of related digital emphasis.

Research and Development   In many industries, an organization cannot grow or even survive without *research and development* (R&D), that organizational function for generating a steady stream of new products and processes. R&D develops new product ideas and nurtures them until the products reach full production and enter the market. The R&D process commonly involves activities like concept generation and screening, product planning and development, and perhaps even test marketing. Some organizations deem R&D a very critical organizational function since new products developed through R&D can be highly profitable and a prerequisite for organizational success.

As its definition implies, in addition to generating new products, in many organizations R&D also includes adding organizational value through improved processes related to activities like manufacturing and marketing. Many organizations use R&D efforts to diligently study how to use progressive concepts like "design for manufacture" or "concurrent engineering" to focus on improving coordination among organizational functions in order to reduce the amount of time it takes for a new product to be fully developed and to reach the market.

Once management understands the specifics of the R&D function in an organization, it is ready to formulate its R&D emphasis on digital strategy. In other words, management is then prepared to develop a plan outlining how digital activities will support the performance of the organization's R&D. Naturally, because R&D activities can vary drastically from organization to organization, digital support for R&D strategy can vary drastically from organization to organization.

Boeing provides an interesting example of using an R&D emphasis in digital strategy. Boeing is one of the world's major aerospace manufacturing firms. The company focuses on commercial airplanes, military aircraft, and space transportation and communication equipment.[2] Recently, Boeing's competitors began using Russian-built rocket engines at sharply discounted prices to gain a competitive price advantage over Boeing's rockets.

Boeing decided to build a new, more efficient and effective R&D process to develop methods to compete with the new lower-cost rocket engines. The heart of the new process was a digital R&D emphasis involving the use of a new extranet to allow concurrent engineering of product parts with suppliers. Boeing's hope in using the new extranet was to make the design phase of the R&D process more efficient and effective. Prior to this extranet, Boeing would essentially contract with a supplier to build a part to predetermined specifications. Through the new extranet, Boeing and its suppliers participated more as partners in a free-flowing, creative process aimed at designing new engine parts.

Boeing's reported results of using its new extranet are dramatic. One product, normally made up of 140 different parts, was redesigned with only 5 parts. The cost of developing an initial version of the product fell from $1.4 million to $50,000. Additionally, design time to develop the product was reduced from 7 man-years to less than 1 man-year. Overall, this digitally focused R&D strategy will help Boeing to be more cost-competitive because its new extranet involving suppliers enabled the company to drastically cut design cycle time, production costs, and design errors.

Operations *Operations* is that organizational function that produces an organization's goods and services. Operations deals with issues in areas like supply-chain management, plant capacity, plant lay-out, manufacturing and production processes, and inventory require-ments. Two important aspects of operations management involve con-trolling costs and improving the efficiency of plant operations. Operations improvement tools include statistical process control, just-in-time inventory methods, continuous improvement systems, and flexible manufacturing systems.

Once management understands the specifics of the operations func-tion in an organization, it is ready to formulate an operations emphasis for its digital strategy. In other words, management is prepared to devel-op a plan outlining how digital activities will support the performance of the operations function. Naturally, because operations activities can vary drastically from organization to organization, digital activity sup-porting operations emphasis can vary drastically from organization to organization.

Digital activities at Honeywell International provide a worthwhile example of an operations emphasis within an organization's digital strat-egy.[3] Honeywell International makes a broad array of aerospace, automation, and transportation products. Honeywell, which plans to sell its automotive products division, has recently agreed to be acquired by industrial giant General Electric.

An operations emphasis is a cornerstone in Honeywell's digital strategy for competing in the Internet economy. In July 1999, Honeywell launched MyPlant.com, a business-to-business Web site that allows customers and suppliers from around the world to share pro-curement strategies and manufacturing strategies, download software, and participate in valuable industry discussions. MyPlant.com con-nects anyone in the manufacturing industry, sometimes even Honeywell competitors. In about the first 15 months of operation, the site hosted over 60,000 user sessions; it is estimated that one-third of the site users were Honeywell customers. Overall, MyPlant.com allows visitors, including Honeywell itself, to collaborate in order to solve crit-ical manufacturing problems.

Recent information indicates that MyPlant.com has been such a huge success that Honeywell plans to initiate MyAircraft.com to focus on supply-chain management for the aerospace industry and MyFacilities.com for the facilities management industry. All three sites are expected to help Honeywell and others to make improvements—for example, improving inventory turns, correcting purchasing inefficien-cies, and reducing overhead.

Finance   Financial specialists in organizations are typically responsible for making forecasts, doing financial planning, evaluating investment proposals, securing financing for various investments, and controlling financial resources. Financial specialists contribute to organizational planning by assessing the potential profit impacts of various planning alternatives, using techniques such as net present value analysis, and evaluating the financial condition of the business.

The role of finance in organizational planning should not be underestimated. Financial analysis answers some of the fundamental questions that drive the planning process. What will it cost to implement a new plan? What financial risk does a new plan present versus continuing the status quo? What method for financing a new plan results in the least cost?

The advent of the Internet has indeed revolutionized the role of financial specialists in organizations. The potential impact of the Internet on the practice of finance in organizations, as with the practice of any other organizational business function, is so profound that financial specialists will undoubtedly have to learn new digital skills to participate acceptably in digital age companies.

Traditionally, financial specialists have been perceived as bean counters.[4] Present as well as future Internet applications, however, will allow such traditional responsibilities as forecasting, budgeting, and financial control to be primarily automated. This automation will provide the organization's financial specialists the time to quantify and critique various planning alternatives to ensure that they create value. In essence, the organization's chief financial specialist will become one of the organization's primary planning consultants.

To allow the financial specialist to become more of an internal planning consultant, financial emphasis in digital strategy can focus on eliminating financial tasks that can be Web-automated. For example, Web applications can be initiated that automate finance transactions from invoicing to payroll. Similarly, Web systems could be employed that allow staff to order goods online directly from suppliers, with real-time financial transaction summaries being made available to appropriate personnel. Financial emphasis in digital strategy can also focus on activities such as those that would allow customers to visit a warehouse and place an order that can be automatically dispatched along with the automatic posting of related accounting transactions on a real-time basis. The net result of such financial emphasis in digital strategy would give financial specialists the time to evaluate planning alternatives, an activity that is valuable to the organization. A possible and likely by-product of this emphasis is to build organizational value through increased efficiency capability.

Marketing   *Marketing* is that organizational function that facilitates the exchange of goods and services between an organization and its customers. Essentially, marketing specialists primarily focus on enabling customers to get products. Marketing specialists determine the appropriate markets in which to offer products, and they develop effective marketing mixes to support the offering. The marketing mix includes four critical elements: determining the product an organization will offer, establishing the price of the product, promoting the product, and selecting the channels for distributing the product. These four elements are controllable variables that marketers use to focus their influence on targeted customers. All four marketing-mix elements should be coordinated to maximize the impact that organizations have on customers.

Once management understands marketing and the specifics of how the marketing function is practiced in a particular organization, it is ready to formulate a marketing emphasis for its digital strategy. In other words, management is prepared to develop a plan outlining how digital activities will support the marketing function.

Reports of managers formulating digital strategies with innovative marketing emphasis are indeed plentiful. Take CIMTEK Medical Company's medicalbuyer.com as an example.[5] To complement its more traditional marketing and sales efforts, CIMTEK decided to establish medicalbuyer.com to compete with several Internet sites that allow doctors and other medical professionals to order medical and surgical products online. Management at CIMTEK believes that medicalbuyer.com has been successful mainly because the site enables doctors to save both time and money. According to estimates, the selling cost and corresponding purchase price of CIMTEK products sold on the Internet can be 15 to 40 percent lower than that of products sold through more traditional methods. CIMTEK expects to build its Internet revenue to the point where it is about 20 to 30 percent of its total revenue. The success of sites like medicalbuyer.com is causing managers throughout the industry to seriously contemplate offering Internet ordering to physicians, thereby somewhat de-emphasizing traditional sales and marketing infrastructure.

Another example of digital strategy with a progressive marketing emphasis involves Lands' End, a direct marketer that offers casual clothing for men, women, and children as well as offering accessories, shoes, and luggage. To build a more personal relationship with customers, the company recently introduced two new programs: Lands' End Live and Shop with a Friend.[6] Available to shoppers at www.landsend.com, Lands' End Live allows customers live, real-time access to personal shopping assistance 24 hours a day, 7 days a week. As they shop, customers can communicate in real time with sales representatives. Questions can be answered through Internet chat format, or a sales representative will quickly call the customer in response to a call request. Shop with a Friend allows customers to shop the Lands' End site with anyone anywhere in the world.

A last example of digital strategy with a marketing emphasis involves the Shell Oil Company.[7] Shell develops, produces, and markets crude oil and natural gas. Recently, Shell management started seeing marketing inconsistencies in the use of its seashell logo in more traditional advertising promotions as well as various company-related Web sites. Management was concerned that such inconsistency would ultimately dilute the impact of Shell's total marketing effort and perhaps even confuse customers about Shell's identity. As a result, the company developed a plan for eliminating the inconsistencies. The plan involved a Web-based extranet that distributes thousands of marketing standards that can easily be updated and customized by marketing staffers and advertising agencies around the world. Essentially, the extranet is a faster and easier means for Shell to manage its marketing efforts than more traditionally published methods.

Human Resource Management   *Human resource management* is that organizational function that focuses on providing appropriate human resources for the organization. In general, the human resource function is concerned with attracting, assessing, motivating, and retaining the employees the firm needs to run effectively. This function is also responsible for activities like employee and management training, affirmative action planning, and evaluation of the safety of the work environment.

Human resource activities are varied and involve focus on factors both inside and outside the organization. External focus, for example, includes tracking developments in laws and regulations that affect employment as well as analyzing changes in the labor market. Internal focus, for example, includes investigating specific problem issues like low productivity, excessive turnover, or high accident rates. In addition, the human resource function can involve internal analysis and proposals for changing organizational structure and climate.

Once management understands the human resource function and the specifics of how this function is practiced in a particular organization, it is ready to formulate a human resource emphasis for its digital strategy. In other words, management is prepared to develop a plan outlining how digital activities will support the performance of the human resource function.

One interesting example of digital strategy with a human resource emphasis involves Aetna, Inc., one of the nation's largest health benefits companies as well as one of the nation's largest insurance and financial services organizations.[8] Employee training at many companies commonly involves transporting employees to central training centers, training employees at those locations, and housing them nearby for overnight stays. Aetna has developed a very different solution to meeting employee training needs. The Aetna solution focuses on training employees online. Aetna has been very active in online training and has trained more than 3000 employees online from 1997 to about 1999. Additionally, Aetna expects to triple its number of people trained online in the very near future.

Results for Aetna's online learning efforts have been impressive. Employees taught online scored 4 percentage points higher on training achievement tests than those taught face-to-face. Aetna discovered that employees seem to retain information much better if it's broken into short modules and presented for learning through interactive digital modules than if presented more traditionally. After software costs, Aetna believes that it has saved $3 million so far through online training. The company plans to expand its online training to employees throughout the customer service area.

Consider Business Operations

Business operations refers to activities supporting an organization or business unit(s) that operates primarily within a single industry. Take Cray, Inc., for example. It operates almost solely in one industry, the supercomputer industry. Cray develops and markets high-performance, general-purpose parallel computer systems. As a result, the emphasis for business operations in Cray's digital strategy should be on providing digital support regarding that one industry and Cray's position in it. Some organizations have a number of business units operating in a single industry. For example, MTV and Nickelodeon are separate units of Viacom that operate in the broadcasting industry. The emphasis for business operations in Viacom's digital strategy should seek to help each of its business units to better compete both individually and collectively in the broadcasting industry.

Three important business operations emphases that can be included within an organization's digital strategy are (1) cost leadership, (2) differentiation, and (3) focus. These emphases are based upon the work of Michael E. Porter, arguably the world's foremost authority on organizational strategy,[9] and are detailed below.

Cost Leadership   *Cost leadership* is a philosophy that focuses on achieving competitive advantage and thus organizational success by gaining acceptable returns through the minimization of costs. Essentially, cost leadership is accomplished through consistent emphasis on efficiency of organizational activities. Cost leadership emphasis aims at helping organizations become low-cost producers in their industries. Digital strategy with a cost leadership emphasis focuses on minimizing organizational costs via digital activities.

An example of digital strategy aimed at lowering operating costs involves Winn-Dixie supermarkets.[10] Talmage Booth, director of corporate energy programs, joined Winn-Dixie in 1997 to prepare the company for electricity deregulation and to develop options for utility cost savings. Early in his tenure at Winn-Dixie, Booth discovered and started using the Cadence Network, an Internet reporting system that enters all of a company's utility information on a secure Internet site. By using the Cadence Network, Booth was able to make sense of the complex array of utilities costs at Winn-Dixie and, as a result, develop logical programs for driving down electric, water, sewer, gas, and liquid propane bills.

Differentiation   *Differentiation* is a philosophy that focuses on marketing unique products that will sell for premium prices. Theoretically, an organization can charge more for such products if consumers think the products are significantly different from others. Perhaps the most differentiated product is a product that is customized or designed specifically for one customer.

Dell Computer has a digital strategy that includes a differentiation emphasis. Dell uses an Internet interface with Ford Motor, one of its large customers, in order to customize products sold to Ford Motor.[11] In essence, Dell creates a number of different computer configurations designed specifically for Ford employees in various departments. When Dell receives an online order via the Ford intranet, it knows immediately what type of worker is ordering and what kind of computer is needed. Based upon this information, Dell assembles the proper hardware and then installs needed software. Some of the software even involves Ford's own code that's stored at Dell.

Naturally, Ford pays somewhat of a premium for Dell's customized products. Without this alternative, however, Ford might be faced with having to purchase its computers from a distributor that would simply send over boxes that need to be unpacked and configured by a Ford technology expert. Such a process can take between 4 and 6 hours and perhaps result in configuration errors that need to be corrected.

Focus *Focus* is a philosophy that emphasizes gaining competitive advantage by segmenting markets and appealing to only one or a few select groups of consumers or organizational buyers. Digital strategy with a focus emphasis limits attention to a few selected customer targets. A firm that adopts such a digital strategy concentrates on one or a few market niches, hoping to serve those niches very well, as opposed to addressing many different types of customers. Examples of products focusing on niches are Rolls-Royce automobiles, Mont Blanc pens, and Hartman luggage. These products are designed to appeal to the upscale market and serve it well rather than trying to compete in the mass market. Not all niche players focus on upscale markets where they can command premium prices. Arguably, Volkswagen's Love Bug and Chrysler's PT Cruiser are examples of products focusing on market niches without charging premium prices.

Consider Corporate Operations

Corporate operations are activities that support the management of a complex corporation as a whole. Digital strategy emphasizing corporate operations supports activities like managing multiple businesses, managing a portfolio of business units across diverse industries, or managing corporate growth. For example, General Electric's portfolio of businesses ranges from jet engines to a television network to light bulbs. From a corporate operations viewpoint, a firm's overarching digital strategy should seek to support these diverse businesses as a synergistic whole.

Major corporate operations commonly include activities in three areas: (1) horizontal integration, (2) vertical integration, and (3) diversification. The following sections describe each of these areas as well as how they might impact digital strategy.

Horizontal Integration   *Horizontal integration* is a philosophy that emphasizes growing an organization by acquiring competing firms in the same line of business. Such a move can quickly increase the size, sales, profits, and potential market share of an organization. Horizontal integration is aimed at increasing market share through acquisition and can be particularly valuable to organizations in slowly growing industries.

Digital strategy with a horizontal integration emphasis can take many different avenues. One of these avenues focuses on facilitating how acquisitions are woven into the business character of an operating concern. For example, Albertson's, one of the largest supermarket and drug chains in the United States, recently purchased three stores from Jitney Jungle Stores of America, Inc., in the greater Memphis, Tennessee, metropolitan area. Digital strategy with a horizontal integration emphasis should focus on incorporating such stores into the digital mainstream of the corporation. As examples, digital strategy emphasizing horizontal integration should focus on such activities as allowing newly purchased stores to use existing corporate digital tools for recruiting new employees, marketing to the local community, and reporting daily store performance to corporate headquarters.

Vertical Integration   *Vertical integration* is a philosophy that emphasizes growing an organization by adding functions previously performed by a supplier or distributor. In a vertically integrated firm, the output of one of the firm's enterprises serves as input for another of the firm's enterprises. For example, a firm that owned both a dairy farm and an ice-cream manufacturer would be vertically integrated if it used the dairy's milk output as input in the production of the ice cream. Theoretically, vertical integration gives greater control over a line of business and increases profits through greater efficiency or better selling efforts.

Like digital strategy with a horizontal integration emphasis, digital strategy with a vertical integration emphasis can take many different avenues. One such avenue focuses on facilitating how vertical integration activities of one organization can be woven into the business character of the umbrella organization. Coordination of vertical activities is a priority. For example, Synnex Technology International Corp. is a distributor of computer products in Taiwan.[12] The company has enjoyed a 20-plus year partnership with Intel and has been a very successful distributor. According to observers, vertical integration is key to Synnex's competitive edge. The company even owns its own delivery trucks. In such a situation, digital strategy with a vertical integration emphasis could involve coordinating such activities as warehousing, sales, delivery, and perhaps even vehicle maintenance if Synnex decided to add maintenance to its vertical integration scheme. Digital components enabling inventory tracking, customer inspection of inventory, customer ordering, delivery scheduling, and even truck maintenance scheduling could all be key in ensuring the success of Synnex's vertical integration activities.

Diversification   *Diversification* is a philosophy that emphasizes building an organization by operating in two or more different industries or with two or more different lines of business. An excellent example of a diversified company is Minnesota Mining and Manufacturing Company (3M). The company offers hundreds of different products in several different industries, including transportation, health care, and business office products. Many of 3M's products represent very different types of businesses operating in different industries. Digital strategy emphasizing diversification commonly focuses on activities such as providing digital means for helping each organizational unit to independently carry out its business and allowing for collaboration across businesses regarding common business challenges. Such emphasis also provides top management with adequate information for controlling diverse business activities both individually and collectively.

Consider Digital Tactics

Previous sections of this chapter suggested that managers consider organizational functions, business operations, and corporate operations when formulating digital strategy. This section advises managers to also consider digital tactics when formulating digital strategy. *Digital tactics* are maneuvers for enhancing the probability that implemented digital strategy will be successful. In essence, digital tactics are characteristics of launched digital strategies.

Several broad or macro digital tactics are commonly employed to enhance the success of digital strategies. For example, managers commonly aim digital activities at generating extra revenue. Such focus can enhance organizational cashflow and ultimately company profitability. As another digital tactic, managers commonly initiate digital activities that reduce costs. Whether helping management to find the lowest-priced materials necessary for product manufacturing, helping sales-people to more efficiently communicate with customers, or helping managers to more effectively schedule workers, digital activities can result in lower operating costs. As a third digital tactic, managers can initiate digital activities that reduce various organizational cycle times. To illustrate, digital applications can reduce product improvement cycle time by accelerating the customer feedback necessary to improve products. Also, digital applications can reduce the organization development cycle by accelerating the online survey administration and analysis necessary to plan and implement organization changes. As still another example of digital tactics, managers can initiate digital activities that increase customer satisfaction. Online customer service can be the catalyst for such increased satisfaction.

In addition to the above more macro digital tactics, managers often employ a number of more micro digital tactics relating to online presence. Although a company marketing manager might employ such tactics, top management should be aware of them as aids in evaluating marketing manager digital efforts. Four such digital tactics with corresponding explanations are to:

- *Make digital presence informative.*   In general, users of Web sites, intranets, and extranets tend to seek and place a high value on discovered information. Such users generally look for many different types of information, including updates of a supplier's policies, new actions taken by competitors, or recent world news. Overall, an online presence that affords access to information that users seek tends to be more satisfying and engaging and therefore used more often and longer than an online presence that does not provide such information. Digital strategy should include a determination of the type(s) of information that site users would be seeking as well as the means for providing that information.

- *Make digital presence efficient.*   In general, users of Web sites, intranets, and extranets tend to seek and place a high value on their time. Such a value seems to indicate that site visitors prefer sites that are quickly and easily navigated. Information that visitors seek should be readily available, clear, and easy to access. Activities like purchasing a product should be quick and intuitive. Employees interfacing with customers who are visiting a site should also find digital tools quick and easy to use. Overall, an online presence that allows visitors to execute their activities efficiently tends to be more satisfying and engaging and therefore used more often and longer than an online presence that does not provide such efficiency. Digital strategy should include steps for making an online presence efficient to use as well as the tactics for providing that efficiency.

- *Make digital presence trustworthy.*   In general, users of Web sites, intranets, and extranets value trustworthy sites. Such a value seems to indicate that visitors prefer sites they can trust. If a site is information-oriented, sources of information should be clearly visible. If site visitors provide personal information in purchasing or being evaluated to purchase a product like a mortgage, they should be assured that the information is confidential. Discussion of encryption technology employed in a site helps customers feel that a site can be trusted. Discussion of topics like a long history of company integrity also helps visitors to trust a site. Providing experts to visitors helps visitors to trust a site. Overall, an online presence that builds a visitor's perception that a site is trustworthy generally tends to be more satisfying and engaging and therefore used more often and longer than online presence that builds visitor perception that a site is untrustworthy. Digital strategy should include steps for building user perception that a site is trustworthy as well as the tactics for building that perception.

- *Make digital presence enjoyable.*   In general, users of Web sites, intranets, and extranets tend to value sites that provide enjoyment. Sites that judiciously use features like humor, games, curious sounds, and engaging graphics can all provide enjoyment to visitors. Overall, an online presence that visitors enjoy tends to be more satisfying and engaging and therefore used more often and longer than an online presence that visitors do not enjoy. Reflecting the digital tactic of making digital presence enjoyable for visitors, digital strategy should include the goal of building visitor enjoyment as well as outlining the steps for reaching that goal.

Managers must understand that the likelihood of digital strategy being successful increases as appropriate digital tactics are included in the strategy. For example, assume that management develops a digital strategy that includes developing an online customer support system. To be successful, the digital strategy must appropriately consider functional, business, and corporate issues. Appropriately considering these issues is certainly a prerequisite for but not a guarantee of the success of this online customer support system. The probability that this digital strategy will be successful can be significantly increased, however, if it includes appropriate digital tactics. That is, as online customer service becomes more informative, efficient, trustworthy, and enjoyable, the probability of the service center being successful increases.

To a large extent, this chapter has focused on many different factors that managers should consider when formulating digital strategy: organizational functions, business operations, corporate operations, and digital tactics. Naturally, the specifics of digital strategy for various organizations will be influenced differently by these factors. It may be advisable for some organizations, depending upon their level of digital involvement, to operate with a digital strategy emphasizing only one or two of these factors. On the other hand, some organizations should probably have a digital strategy that emphasizes many of these factors.

Digital Strategy: Comprehensiveness and Value Added

Comprehensive digital strategy is digital strategy that addresses a significant proportion of the digital opportunities available to an organization. Explaining why managers should strive to develop digital strategy that is as comprehensive as possible is simple indeed. The more comprehensive an organization's digital strategy, the more value that strategy adds to the organization. Naturally digital strategy leads to higher organizational value only when such a strategy is implemented successfully. Figure 6.2 illustrates this relationship between digital strategy comprehensiveness and organizational value. The figure depicts various digital strategies that, when considered cumulatively, can contribute to increasing digital strategy comprehensiveness as well as organizational value. Take note that the digital strategies depicted in Figure 6.2 are for example purposes only. Depending upon specific organizational circumstances, perhaps radically different digital strategies can and should

Figure 6.2 Sample digital strategies that can increase both digital strategy comprehensiveness and the value of an organization.

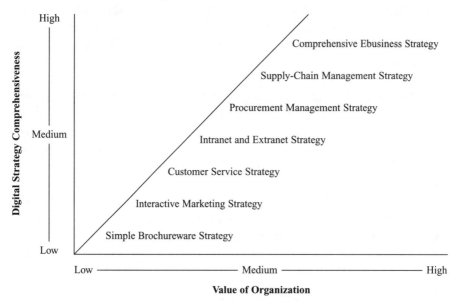

be formulated to increase digital strategy comprehensiveness and corresponding organizational value.

In discussing Figure 6.2, an organization's total digital strategy might consist of brochureware. This level of digital strategy comprehensiveness is most likely drastically incomplete for most organizations and would result in very little added value for the organization. As ingredients related to issues like interactive marketing, customer service, intranets, and extranets are added to digital strategy, however, both digital strategy comprehensiveness and organizational value increase. Managers must keep in mind that Figure 6.2 does *not* claim that comprehensiveness necessarily starts with simple brochureware and then moves to interactive marketing, then to customer service, and so forth. This figure *does* claim, however, that progressive and cumulative additions to digital strategy tend to increase digital strategy comprehensiveness and company value. In other words, the order in which digital opportunities are addressed is probably not as important as management's commitment to comprehensively and continually take advantage of the opportunities.

Hilton Hotels Corporation provides one of the best examples of a company constantly adding to its value by continually enhancing digital strategy comprehensiveness. The company, which has over 1800 hotels worldwide, seems to be continually building and implementing digital activities to take advantage of more opportunities.[13] One of Hilton's newest digital thrusts focuses on allowing customers to access company ebusiness systems through mobile phone access.

Ebusiness became a priority at Hilton in 1995. Since then, the company has made outstanding progress in putting digital activities into operation. Hilton was one of the first in its industry to offer bookings over the Internet and provide business reservations services through extranets, and it does about 30 percent of its $1 billion annual procurement online. According to reports, ebusiness systems have allowed Hilton to significantly increase its customer base, sell and collect payments online, increase revenue via ebusiness transactions, and significantly reduce costs in the areas of materials procurement, customer management, and order fulfillment.

Back to American Airlines

This section illustrates how digital dimensioning principles apply to real organizations. Consider the following information as digital dimensioning advice that an ebusiness consultant might have given American Airlines management as input for initiating its digital presence. To gain maximum benefit from this section, explore aa.com before reading further.

"As management at American Airlines, you must understand that a major step in building ebusiness success at American is developing an effective digital strategy. Essentially, this digital strategy would be your master plan for outlining how American's digital activities will fulfill your statement of digital direction as well as digital support goals. As you know, since your statement of digital direction and your digital support goals are consistent with American's purpose and overall goals, digital strategy literally helps the organization to be successful.

"Formulate your digital strategy to gain advantage over competitors like Delta and United. To do this, consider the functions performed at American. These functions would include activities like your marketing efforts, human resource efforts, and flying operations. Develop a digital strategy that supports the performance of these activities at American.

"When formulating digital strategy, also consider business operations at American. Can digital strategy support emphases on cost leadership, differentiation, or focus at American? Reflect on how digital activities can support cost savings efforts, help to make flying with American different from flying with competitors, or address the needs of a particular customer group like traveling families or senior citizen travelers. Since American is arguably an organization operating in a particular line of business, business operations issues will probably be very relevant in formulating an effective digital strategy for your company.

"When formulating digital strategy at American, think about corporate operations. Perhaps your digital strategy should address horizontal integration issues, vertical integration issues, and/or diversification issues. Perhaps you need to perform activities like integrating newly purchased airline companies into your way of doing business. Perhaps you need to integrate a fuel company that will provide jet fuel for your business operations. Perhaps you need to manage a company unrelated to the airline business, like a fast-food chain, which you bought to diversify your company. Digital strategy can be aimed at supporting all such activities.

"When formulating your digital strategy, also consider employing micro digital tactics, to enhance the success of your digital strategy. Such tactics could include having a digital presence that is packed with useful information, convenient to use, trustworthy, and enjoyable to use. People will be encouraged to experience American's digital presence the more tactics of this sort characterize the presence.

"Overall, be comprehensive in building American's digital strategy. That is, make use of the wide array of digital application opportunities that you have. Digital strategy should continually evolve at American Airlines, taking advantage of new digital application possibilities as they arise. Remember, the more comprehensive your digital strategy for American Airlines, the more value that strategy adds to American Airlines."

Digital Dimensioning Resolutions

- Make sure that everyone in your organization understands the meaning of *digital strategy*.

- In formulating digital strategy, emphasize how the organization will exist in the future.

- In formulating digital strategy, emphasize gaining competitive advantage.

- When formulating digital strategy, consider functions of the organization.

- When formulating digital strategy, consider business operations.

- When formulating digital strategy, consider corporate operations.

- When formulating digital strategy, consider digital tactics.

- Design a digital strategy for your organization that appropriately combines and reflects tactical, functional, business operations, and corporate operations issues.

- Make your digital strategy as comprehensive as possible—taking advantage of as many opportunities as possible.

- Formulate digital strategy to add value to the organization.

chapter 7

Implementing Digital Strategy

Executive Preview

This chapter provides a detailed explanation of implementing digital strategy, the process of putting digital strategy into action. The process of putting digital strategy into action is thoroughly explained with the understanding that even the most sound of ebusiness strategies is subject to failure without appropriate implementation practices. The chapter begins by describing the implementation practices of Bristol-Myers Squibb Co., a highly successful company in the old economy whose implementation of a well-designed digital strategy has positioned it for even greater success in the new economy. Next, the chapter introduces the fundamentals of implementing digital strategy and describes its core considerations. Because implementation necessitates swift and judicious action, a discussion of proper planning follows. Implementation planning includes issues of prioritization, timing, and resource allocation. The chapter then looks at the issues involved in putting the implementation plan into action. These considerations include schedule adherence, communication facilitation, testing, prelaunch planning, and launch. Returning to Bristol-Myers Squibb, the following section of the chapter contains advice a consultant would have given company management while considering steps to putting its digital strategy into action. The chapter concludes with a list of resolutions that managers can follow when implementing digital strategies.

Bristol-Myers Squibb Co.[1]

Bristol-Myers Squibb Co. is an $18.3 billion maker of personal care products and over-the-counter pharmaceuticals. The organization has produced and marketed popular household brands like Bufferin, Excedrin, Nuprin, and Keri lotion for several decades. With its international infrastructure, fickle marketplace, and competitive industry, Bristol-Myers has a broad array of considerations in formulating and refining its digital strategy. And the challenge of continually implementing that strategy calls for an entirely different set of responsibilities than those needed in formulating and refining strategy.

Many of the company's implementation activities are championed by the organization's chief information officer (CIO), Jack Cooper. Cooper coordinates implementation activities with a firm grasp of the organization's business priorities. According to Cooper, though, the role of a CIO is particularly challenging because of the sporadic and dynamic nature of implementing multiple projects concurrently. "You have to know how to commit resources and set deadlines and know when perfect is too costly," Cooper explains.

In addition to the managerial skills of implementing digital strategies, Cooper continues, facilitating implementation activities requires certain leadership faculties as well. Motivation is particularly critical. "It's easy to have a reason why the project won't meet its current obligation. You have to get past those to succeed. The desire to win and to create solutions in the face of adversity—that has to be promoted, encouraged, and worked on all the time." The philosophy and attitude of Cooper and Bristol-Myers Squibb are certainly judicious. Clearly, the implementation perspective of the company is a thoughtful one. Bristol-Myers understands that the same high level of conceptualization that goes into formulating digital strategy must go into implementing it as well.

Principles for Implementing Digital Strategy

What's Ahead? The Spotlight described circumstances at Bristol-Myers Squibb where significant steps had already been taken by management to formulate its ebusiness strategy. Digital strategy had likely been developed with the core objectives of the organization firmly in mind. From this point, the next step for management at Bristol-Myers Squibb was to put these strategies into action. This chapter will describe a series of considerations and steps for doing just that in your organization.

Fundamentals of Implementing Digital Strategy

Undoubtedly, the digital dimensioning process is a contemplative and thoughtful one. The first step, enlisting digital expertise, ensures that the organization will have the appropriate human resources involved in digital activities. The second step, analyzing the organization's digital environment, reinforces the idea that digital activities must be carefully planned with respect to environmental factors. The third step, establishing digital direction, helps the organization to clarify its goals and objectives. The fourth step, described in the previous chapter, guides the organization in formulating the strategy to pursue its digital direction. The next area of focus shifts to the process of putting digital strategy into action, the subject of this chapter. The same level of contemplation that goes into formulating digital strategy must be applied to its execution as well. This chapter specifically addresses these contemplative issues and guides management in taking hold of its digital strategy and carrying out proper implementation.

Implementation in and of itself is an issue that is often overlooked. Indeed a critical business function, implementation is in many cases responsible for the success or failure of business initiatives. It is a commonly held notion that entrepreneurial success does *not* necessarily hinge on the generation of an idea but on the execution of that idea. Many people can develop an idea for a new product or even an entire business. But the mark of a successful entrepreneur is in his or her ability to *plan* implementation, secure the required resources, and maintain the commitment to see it through. Just as for a start-up business, achieving ebusiness success depends in large part upon the execution of a sound plan. In the context of digital dimensioning, this "plan" is the formulated digital strategy. Still, simply *having* a formidable strategy is not enough. An organization must have an equally sound plan for actually putting the strategy into action and pursuing success. Following the order of the digital dimensioning model, a formulated digital strategy will be the foundation of implementation. For an organization to effectively cross the bridge between the formulation and implementation of digital strategy, managers must be sure the strategy itself is properly articulated and disseminated.

Documentation

Documenting the digital strategy of an organization is an important task of management. A digital strategy should, in some form, be put into a document that comprehensively outlines functions, business operations, corporate operations, and digital tactics, as described in Chapter 6. Serious consideration should be given to the sensitivity of such documentation, though. Since some aspects of a digital strategy will likely be competitor-oriented, it is obviously important that the content of the strategy be protected. The length and content of a digital strategy document will vary from one organization to another. Managers may choose to complement a comprehensive digital strategy with an executive summary. A shorter executive summary document will be both more palatable to many in the organization and safer for general circulation. Consider making the document available on the company intranet and/or distributing it to the entire organization via email.

Disseminating and Articulating Digital Strategy

Managers must also consider supplementary tactics to clarify or reinforce the documented digital strategy. Such tactics include corporate events where executives can present the strategy and explain its various aspects to the entire company and informal "brown-bag" lunches where managers can discuss the strategy with various members of the organization. Since many are likely to have questions and comments, it is probably a good idea to complement formal presentations with informal interactive settings. The act of articulating an organization's digital strategy should not be overlooked or sidestepped. Ensuring that the entire organization understands the strategy will greatly improve the likelihood of successful implementation. The reasons for this will be discussed both later in this chapter regarding change management and in the final chapter of the book concerning organizational culture in the new economy.

Planning for the Implementation of Digital Strategy

Once the strategy is documented and understood throughout the organization, the process of implementation truly begins. Like any considerable organizational endeavor, planning is critical. Implementation planning, the process of scheduling and prioritizing implementation activities, is the first step in implementation.

Poorly planned implementation can result in schedule or investment overruns and mistiming. Given the nature of Internet speed, the effects of misarranged activities can be disastrous in terms of market opportunities, competitive maneuvers, or both.

Prioritization

Implementation planning begins with the process of prioritization. Because not all aspects of an organization's digital strategy can be addressed simultaneously, managers must determine which ones should be addressed first. Working with different members of the organization's digital expertise, conceptual experts should take the lead in prioritizing different elements of the organization's digital strategy. Conceptual experts should determine priorities based upon a variety of factors. Most often these factors will be market demands or competitive pressures. The digital strategy should be examined in great detail for those areas that seem to represent priorities in these respects. Luckily, the top priorities are often very recognizable. For example, suppose a regional courier service called Old World Couriers is losing market share to its chief competitor, Jiffy Ship, which offers customers free use of an online package tracking system. Old World's analysis of its digital environment would likely conclude that customers that recently regarded Web-based tracking as a novel feature now view it as a necessary item and expectation. In this case, Old World should place a high priority on building a comparable tracking system due to market demands and competitive pressure. Failing to address this issue as a high priority could be fatal to the future of the business. For reasons like this one, organizations should take steps to determine priorities. Even though Old World's digital strategy may call for a number of important initiatives, management should take steps to identify *top* priorities.

Timing

Once implementation priorities are determined, the organization must discuss issues of timing. With respect to implementation, the most important aspects of timing are scheduling and phasing. Scheduling refers basically to establishing a timetable for the design, development, testing, and launch of digital applications. Market demands for applications like online package tracking are so intense that the pressure to make them available to customers is enormous. Every day that Old World goes without an online tracking system is another opportunity for Jiffy Ship to win new customers. But building and deploying applications that meet a strategic need can be very time-consuming. For this reason, an organization must be mindful of the phased approach to application development.

Let us assume that the package tracking system offered by Jiffy Ship includes package tracking, pick-up scheduling, supplies reordering, and payment processing. Technical and people experts at Old World have determined that it will require 9 months to build an application with these four features and train employees how to use it. Conceptual experts, though, determine that the market impact of *not* having the application for this amount of time will be disastrous. The solution to the problem is found in the notion of project phasing. Too often, organizations try to build and deploy too much at one time, even though the timetable for doing so can be deadly to the opportunity.

As part of implementation planning, Old World should develop multiple phases of the project so that some—not all—of the application functions can be rolled out and made available to customers. If market research indicates that even though four features of the application are offered, only package tracking and supplies reordering are the ones being used by customers to any significant degree, Old World should consider developing a phased implementation schedule whereby these two features are made available to customers as soon as possible. The technical and people experts would likely conclude that focusing on only two features now would require a much shorter timetable. Additional application features could be rolled out to customers in a later phase.

Resource Allocation

Once an implementation plan's scheduling and phasing issues are addressed, management must address the issue of resource allocation. Resource allocation, in the context of implementing digital strategy, refers to resource planning and to the securing of those resources necessary to successfully put digital strategy into action. In this regard, management must determine what resources will be required and for what duration. Most often, the scarcest resource is time. Old World may determine that the modified project's duration will only take 4 months. However, this assumes that there are no other internal projects currently being implemented and/or that external experts are not committed to other clients. This may present a set of resource conflicts internally and externally. If so, management must either resolve conflicts to have resources available during the needed times or seek external resources to compensate.

Another important resource to consider is capital, especially if your efforts will require a significant degree of external expertise or new hardware or software. Capital expenditures are not as likely if the majority of implementation will be handled by existing personnel and the existing hardware and software infrastructure. Planning for capital expenditures should be done in conjunction with conceptual experts and members of the organization's finance team. From the perspective of cash expenditures, be sure that those with check-signing authority understand the project phases and payment schedules. In many cases, cash outlay is the fuel of ebusiness motion. Be sure that financial resources are secured as part of the implementation plan.

Resource allocation must work in concert with implementation prioritization and timing. These three aspects together constitute a vital part of implementing digital strategy: planning. Planning is generally understood to be a critical business function in and of itself. The pressure of Internet speed makes it particularly critical in terms of the digital dimensioning process.

The by-product of implementation planning is a tangible implementation plan. The plan should include delivery dates, resource schedules, and project update meetings. Since various organizations handle internal projects differently and have individual processes for formulating development schedules, the deliverable item itself can take many different shapes. Whether the plan is on a mural wall calendar, online groupware engine, or printed Gantt chart, the plan should be tangible and dispersed to the appropriate personnel.

Execution: Carrying Out the Implementation Plan

Following the process of implementation planning, the organization moves to actually performing the tasks at hand. This aspect of implementation is called execution, and it generally involves putting the implementation plan into action. Execution is perhaps the *least* conceptual area of the entire digital dimensioning process. It involves less thinking and more doing. However, managers must guide the execution process along in many respects.

The implementation plan will no doubt include marching orders for various members of the organization. Technical experts begin writing the code, installing hardware, and configuring software for different applications and features. People and conceptual experts begin to develop user interface designs, write process documents, and create application help and support documentation. While things are progressing, there are several considerations for managers. The most critical of these are schedule adherence, communication facilitation, and morale monitoring.

Schedule Adherence

First of all, managers must be constantly aware of implementation progress with respect to the implementation plan. The scarcest resource will probably be time allocation of those involved. As important as ebusiness activities are to the organization, there will likely be other responsibilities for technical personnel that may prevent them from dedicating necessary time to the various ebusiness projects at hand. As a manager, it is critical to detect these instances early and make necessary adjustments. Failure to do so could result in serious delays in the schedule and delivery dates.

In addition to the schedule of actual activities, management must closely watch the development of various activities and be sure that the personnel involved are in sync. Individuals working on different parts of an initiative will naturally work in isolation throughout a project. This can be counterproductive in many respects, though. If a technical expert encounters a programming issue that raises potential usability questions, he or she should consult a people expert to determine the best resolution. Failure to do so might result in a decision that hinders the end product.

Returning to the Old World Couriers example, assume that 2 weeks into developing the online tracking system a technical expert has a question about the customer sign-in process. By default the technical programmer assumes that the log-in screen will require a customer's account number and personal identification number (PIN). The logic behind this decision seems reasonable enough. Various people experts know full well, though, that most of Old World's customers don't know their account number. When they call by telephone to place an order currently, customer service representatives locate the accounts by referencing the customers' telephone numbers. If this disparity is encountered early enough, the programmer can design the phone number sign-in from the start. If it is detected upon project completion, though, the adjustment might consume several weeks and consequently delay the application's launch.

Facilitating Team Communication

Management must facilitate communication and collaboration among various areas of the project team. Project segments done in complete isolation can create significant delays in the successful completion of the project. A manager should certainly initiate and facilitate various cross-functional milestone meetings whereby multiple personnel can communicate about issues like the one at Old World. An advisable supplement to formal meetings might be informal gatherings such as lunches or happy hours where various project nuances can be discussed.

Monitoring Team Morale

Building on this issue of collaboration and communication among the different team areas is the notion of the team dynamic itself. Since the nature of ebusiness execution is often deadline-driven and functionally challenging, management must carefully monitor the effects of these circumstances within project teams. Bear in mind that such adverse factors can produce negative effects upon the dynamics of a team. Management should anticipate and preempt such negative consequences by addressing team difficulties early and building morale continually. Being conscious of such issues can help to reinforce a positive team dynamic and foster project success.

Preparing for Launch

In addition to monitoring project milestones, facilitating team communication, and monitoring team dynamics, management must prepare and manage testing and other prelaunch activities. Regardless of the quality of personnel and resources assigned to the project, management must assume that there will be problems in the produced applications. The nature of application development is very intense and involved.

Because of this, many of the people working on a project have been working with the code and documentation so long that they are unable to see problems. In design and programming this is commonly referred to as "being too close" to a project. Be sure that applications are subject to internal scrutiny and testing. Figure 7.1 contains a list of questions that the organization should ask about the operability of the project or application before it is officially launched.

Managers should expect problems and be sure that sufficient time is allocated to fix them properly. If Old World launches a faulty tracking system and the customers experience problems, it would likely reinforce their decision to switch to Jiffy Ship. Be sure that small bugs or errors do not diminish all the resources invested in an ebusiness activity.

Perhaps concurrently with testing, managers should be conscious of a number of other prelaunch items. First and foremost, it is important to be sure that the appropriate members of the organization are fully versed in the operation of applications. No matter how simple an application might be to use, assume that customers are going to call by telephone for assistance with some facets. When this occurs, it is critical that sup-

Figure 7.1 Prelaunch questions and considerations.

- Will someone without previous exposure to the application understand how it works?

- Are help and support resources extensive and available?

- Is the design of the interface user-friendly?

- Are visual consistencies present in design and alignment?

- Do usernames and passwords function properly?

- Does the application conform to acceptable online norms and standards?

- Will the application work in different software and operating system environments?

- Do common functions and procedures of the application work properly?

- Is the system free of error messages?

port personnel are able to provide the necessary help to customers. In addition to the technical aspects of applications, educate all personnel about customer concerns such as future product enhancements. In the case of Old World, management should be sure to communicate to customer service representatives that while only two features of the application are currently available, two more are expected shortly.

Next, management should consult with conceptual experts to be sure that the implications of the application launch are fully considered and anticipated. The launch must be fully communicated to customers and media so they understand the impact. Some employees may feel threatened by the introduction of new technology that diminishes their role or value to the organization. Be prepared to effectively communicate with employees about such issues. Additionally, ensure that related marketing materials and documentation will be ready for dissemination in conjunction with application launch.

Launch

Then the exciting time to officially launch applications to internal and external customers will arrive. Depending on the nature of the application and routines of an organization's corporate communications, announce the launch to target constituents. Make them aware that the application is available and explain its features and benefits.

Beyond an external perspective, consider internal issues as well. First of all, be sure that appropriate (if not all) members of the organization are aware of the launch. In the process of doing so, consider this an opportunity to recognize those who played instrumental roles in the project. At the same time, management should reinforce the organization's digital direction and strategy that spawned the application itself. Old World management should remind the organization of the competitive implications that motivated it to undertake the online tracking project. Since ebusiness is a philosophy and not an episode, use launches as springboards to future modifications and projects.

Lastly, celebrate. Launch parties—whether an involved reception where customers and media are invited or an informal gathering to reward the project team—are ideal ways to celebrate. Consider the launch party of iwon.com, an Internet search engine that gives cash prizes to selected users that visit the company Web site. The company's business model is based in part upon awarding one user per month a $1 million cash prize. During the firm's launch party in 1999, employees and guests mingled in a large room with a guarded $1 million cash prize in the center of the room. The company used the event to promote the business to customers and energize employees and suppliers. Many deadline-driven projects create significant stress and fatigue within involved team members. It is not uncommon for project team members to work weekends or evenings to bring an application to market on time. Use the launch as a time to let team members relax and blow off steam. They will likely need it to recover from their long hours on the project. At the same time, managers should use launch parties as morale boosters going into future projects where the same intensity will surely be needed.

Simply put, execution is the motion that's driven by the steps of digital dimensioning. From a management perspective, though, successful execution requires an approach that is conceptually sound. The role of management is to ensure that the coordination of expert roles, allocated resources, and implementation scheduling is sound. Given this notion, management must thoughtfully consider its implementation activities before, during, and after the process itself.

Leadership in the Digital Arena

The process of implementation will no doubt present unique circumstances for managers. Performing the analysis of an organization's digital environment, assembling its digital expertise, establishing its digital direction, and formulating its digital strategy are highly conceptual activities that will likely be very manageable, given management's commitment to diligently following the process. Implementation, though, can be particularly challenging to a manager, given the many unexpected circumstances that may ensue.

The final topic for discussion in this chapter will focus on the leadership considerations of managers fostering the process of implementing digital strategy. Many voices in the new economy are emphasizing the important differences between management and leadership. As a term, *leadership* has developed a more positive connotation than *management*, a slightly different function with several common elements. In fact, the two terms are commonly used interchangeably. Leadership, though, is actually a function of management. Chapter 2 outlined the five functions of management in the new economy: planning, organizing, influencing, controlling, and digital dimensioning. Leadership issues are in large part functions of influence.

Different managers in an organization have varying degrees of leadership skills. Some individuals are sound leaders but poor managers. They can effectively influence others in the organization but fall short in planning or organizing, for example. Other managers are fully versed in management principles but are unable to lead. These individuals are deficient in the area of influence for one reason or another.

Ebusiness success, though, involves the embodiment of the management techniques outlined throughout the digital dimensioning process *and* positive leadership attributes. Leadership prowess is particularly critical during implementation. This aspect of the digital dimensioning process is subject to many variables and challenges, depending upon an organization's strategy, its marketplace conditions, its financial resources, and its technology infrastructure. Regardless of the depth and breadth of technical and managerial experience involved in strategy formulation, implementation will likely reveal unforeseeable difficulties or hurdles. Formulated strategies seem very concise and clairvoyant. Putting the strategy into action, though, typically presents several ambiguous challenges. Because of the dynamic nature of implementation scenarios, there is no comprehensive prescription for how to handle every instance of difficulty or for which option to choose when faced with a variety of alternatives. Instead, a number of general management hurdles will be presented along with leadership considerations of each. The example of Old World Couriers will be used again to describe practical examples of these hurdles.

Logistical Hurdles

One of the more common implementation hurdles deals with logistical considerations. Logistics simply refers to the systems and processes that must be in place to carry out business functions and/or deliver value to customers. Logistics must be established and defined for nearly every aspect of an organization's operations. The lack of proper logistics can result in inconsistency, waste, and internal confusion.

New ebusiness initiatives often generate a host of logistical questions that must be addressed by a variety of organizational members. Returning to the efforts of Old World and its creation of a Web-based package tracking system, suppose that during implementation an important issue of logistics rose. One of the company's conceptual experts realizes that reliance on a Web-based tracking system will eliminate a critical information component. Currently, customer service representatives typically use phone tracking sessions to proactively verify and update customer addresses and billing information. Moving to a Web-based system will eliminate this opportunity for company representatives.

From a leadership perspective, it is important to guide team members through the process of solving such problems and overcoming hurdles. Managers should facilitate communication within the company to determine ways to address the issue. Managers should also encourage the involved parties whose work may have been set back by the surfacing of logistical hurdles.

Human Relations Hurdles

Implementation is also likely to create instances of conflict between different team members or organizational departments. There are multiple factors that can create such conflicts. Typically, the first conflict is a turf war. Oftentimes, ebusiness applications are created by a team that may not include members from *every* area of the organization. If an application has an effect upon, say, the human resources department but no individual from that area is involved in the digital planning or strategy discussions, implementation will come as somewhat of a surprise to those in that area. It is understandably unsettling to members of the organization when decisions about their jobs are made without their input. This "unsettling" feeling can evolve into anger, dissension, or resentment if not handled properly.

A leader's role in this instance is to help resolve conflict. The most desirable action, of course, is to prevent conflict before it occurs. This is not always possible, though. So when conflict does occur, a leader must take steps to quickly dissolve the circumstances that can create a potentially counter-productive implementation environment. Start by understanding the situation and providing a healthy opportunity for upset parties to explain and voice their frustration. Listen empathetically and genuinely. Continue by apologizing (if appropriate) for failing to include the parties in the discussion and propose realistic solutions that accommodate both the people and the business objectives.

A leader must champion the process of implementing digital strategy by being conscious of not only the technology and strategy but the organization's people as well. Ebusiness initiatives often call for change. And change often causes stress for both the organization and its members. Anticipate the stress and be creative in proposing remedies.

Technical Hurdles

Perhaps the most nebulous of implementation challenges are those of a technical nature. The development of some applications sometimes presents technical roadblocks that could seriously hamper implementation progress and schedules. As a result, some applications must be rewritten or reengineered to achieve the original objective.

When this occurs, management must react as quickly as possible to accommodate for the altered circumstances. From a leadership perspective, a manager must effectively communicate the altered schedule to others in the organization. If the technical hurdle has created a delay in the launch date, that must be communicated to others so that other prelaunch and launch activities can be adjusted accordingly.

From the standpoint of technical personnel addressing the hurdle itself, it is important to be as encouraging and accommodating as possible. Sometimes, technical hurdles do not have clear remedies. Difficulties with an application are often bewildering to programmers and require tactical research and investigation to discover possible solutions. In these cases, management must ensure that technical personnel are equipped with adequate resources to solve these problems. Proactively offer to help in securing alternative resources such as additional capital, personnel, or technical resources. While many managers may not necessarily be able to help in solving the technical problem itself, they may indeed be able to help in finding or acquiring solution sources. During these times, a leader should be sure to be present and/or available after hours if necessary. A leader who steps away from the problem can seriously injure morale.

Managers who undertake the challenges and responsibilities of the digital dimensioning process must understand the importance of leadership during every step—especially implementation. Implementation will most likely present team members with unique challenges, uncertainties, and frustrations. The manager must use leadership faculties throughout the process to guide the organization over implementation hurdles and enjoy the fruits of its success. A sound digital strategy requires thoughtful implementation. Managers must articulate the strategy, plan the implementation, and manage execution. Even the best of digital strategies is nearly worthless to the organization if not implemented effectively.

Back to Bristol-Myers Squibb

This section will apply critical chapter concepts to the opening case of the chapter. Consider the following information as digital dimensioning advice that a consultant might have given Bristol-Myers Squibb management as input for managing the process of implementation as directed by the organization's digital strategy.

"As management at Bristol-Myers Squibb, you are to be commended on the merits of your digital strategy. It is certainly comprehensive and precise and reflects a high level of conceptual focus. The main components of your digital strategy reflect an intensive study of your organization's digital environment and a commitment to determining a sound direction. At the outset, be advised that putting your digital strategy into action will require the same high level of conceptual thinking.

"First and foremost, be sure that your digital strategy is well documented and articulated throughout the organization. The more people understand and support the digital strategy, the greater the chances are for implementation success. Following the strategy's articulation and dissemination, begin the process of implementation planning. Since implementation will likely require a multitude of resources and time constraints, solid planning is critical. Be sure to prioritize initiatives, consider phased scheduling, and begin securing required resources as soon as possible.

"Once the implementation plan is established, execution begins. During this time, be sure that the schedule is being followed as closely as possible. Implementation delays could have serious ramifications for other areas of the organization. Because implementation will involve different areas of the organization, be sure to facilitate communication so that project components are not developed independently of one another. In addition, monitor the tone and morale of those working together on the project. Whenever possible, take action to encourage a positive tone within the team and to foster a high level of morale.

"Lastly, lead. Implementation will require that management places special emphasis on people. Team members will undoubtedly encounter hurdles and difficulties that will require your guidance and support. Be prepared to guide the organization through these challenges using faculties of leadership and influence. Your digital strategy is clearly sound and well developed. Be as diligent in implementing it as you were in formulating it."

Digital Dimensioning Resolutions

- Be sure that your digital strategy is clearly articulated throughout your enterprise.

- Be as thoughtful in considering the implementation of digital strategy as you were in conceiving it.

- Since various components of a digital strategy are not all necessarily equal in importance, consider the high priorities first when planning implementation.

- Make sure all resources are in place before beginning implementation.

- Throughout implementation, take steps to continually monitor project progress with respect to the implementation plan.

- Be sure to facilitate formal and informal communication during implementation.

- Closely monitor and adjust team morale over the course of implementation.

- Be mindful of internal and external prelaunch considerations.

- Embody positive leadership attributes to complement the management aspect of the digital dimensioning process.

- Negotiate implementation hurdles tactfully by using common leadership principles.

chapter 8

Controlling Digital Dimensioning

Executive Preview

This chapter tells managers what they need to know to control digital dimensioning. Digital dimensioning control is a special type of organizational control that focuses on monitoring, evaluating, and, when necessary, improving the digital dimensioning process to make sure that it functions properly. In reading this chapter managers will learn about how to measure digital performance since measuring digital performance is an essential part of digital dimensioning control. Managers will also gain insights about controlling digital dimensioning by examining the mistakes of failed dotcoms. The chapter opens with a discussion that highlights digital activity at Procter & Gamble, and comes full turn by closing with a discussion that offers digital dimensioning advice that a consultant could have given Procter & Gamble management as input for establishing its digital activities. The chapter ends with a list of resolutions that you can make to enhance the ebusiness competitiveness of *your* organization.

The Internet Is High Profile in Procter & Gamble's New Push[1]

The Procter & Gamble Company (P&G), headquartered in Cincinnati, Ohio, is a world-renowned manufacturer and marketer of consumer products. The array of products offered by the company is wide and includes household names like Tide laundry detergent, Folgers coffee, Secret anti-perspirant, Downy fabric softener, Crest toothpaste, and Ivory soap.

Since William Procter and James Gamble started P&G in 1837, the company has been very proactive and has focused on the goal of doubling sales every decade. Although historically the company has been largely successful in reaching this sales-doubling goal, in more recent times the target has been in jeopardy. Annual sales growth has been slowing over the last few years, from about a 5 percent increase in 1996 to about a 2.5 percent increase in 1999.

A. G. Lafley, recently appointed as Procter & Gamble's new CEO, is charged with the mandate of reaching this sales-doubling goal. To carry out this mandate, Lafley will likely support the "spirit" of a program he inherited called Organization 2005. This program focuses on revitalizing P&G's recent stagnant sales growth through innovation and product improvement. Overall, Organization 2005 aims at changing P&G's company culture from a conservative, slow-moving bureaucracy to a modern, fast-moving, Internet-savvy organization. The company needs to make faster and better decisions, cut red tape, and fuel innovation better.

The catalyst for overhauling the P&G culture is technology. The company is spending $1 billion annually on technology improvements. New technology initiatives include establishing online collaborative technology to facilitate planning and marketing, business-to-consumer ecommerce systems, Web-based relationships with P&G's supply chain, and decision systems that deliver timely data to P&G desktops worldwide.

Procter & Gamble is obviously building a digital dimensioning thrust that relates to many different areas of operations. Managers must keep in mind, however, that thoughtful digital dimensioning plans are a necessary but not a sufficient condition for digital success at P&G. In addition to sound digital dimensioning plans, management must control digital dimensioning activities to produce the intended results.

Principles of Digital Dimensioning Control

What's Ahead? The Spotlight discussed a newly developed, innovative digital thrust at Procter & Gamble. Essentially, this new digital thrust involves establishing an array of digital applications to support company operations. These new applications include the establishment of new business-to-business ecommerce systems, new Web-based relationships with suppliers, and new worldwide dissemination to managers of critical decision-related information. Certainly, such digital plans could significantly enhance Procter & Gamble's future. In the end, however, the value of such plans will rely on the company's ability to control digital dimensioning, or make sure that these digital applications actually materialize as planned. Managers like those at Procter & Gamble will find valuable insights in this chapter about how to control digital dimensioning.

Introduction

Step 1 of the digital dimensioning process is enlisting digital expertise. After digital expertise has been enlisted, the digital dimensioning process continues with step 2, using this expertise to analyze the organization's digital environment. Armed with information discovered during this analysis, management takes step 3 of the digital dimensioning process, establishing the organization's digital direction. Next, steps 4 and 5 of the process are, respectively, formulating digital strategy and implementing digital strategy. This chapter focuses on the last step of the digital dimensioning process, controlling digital dimensioning. This step ensures that every step in the digital dimensioning process performs as anticipated.

Controlling Organizations

Managers must understand the broader issues involved in controlling organizations before they can fully appreciate the special issues that arise in controlling digital dimensioning. Overall, controlling an organization involves monitoring, evaluating, and improving various activities that take place within an organization. The following sections focus on the broader concept of controlling organizations by defining *control* and outlining the steps of the controlling process. This broader coverage of control ultimately evolves into a more narrow discussion of controlling digital dimensioning later in this chapter.

Defining Control

Every manager must control. *Control* means to make something happen the way it was planned to happen.[2] For example, if an organization plans to increase sales by 25 percent based upon a new, improved product, control entails monitoring progress and making organizational modifications, if necessary, to ensure that sales actually increase by 25 percent.

In order to control effectively, a manager must have a clear idea of the results that a particular action should generate. Then the manager can determine if the desired results are materializing and make any necessary changes to ensure that they do indeed materialize. Since managers control to make sure that plans become reality, they need a clear picture of expected results.

The Control Process

Managers control by following three steps: measuring performance, comparing measured performance with standards (planned results), and improving activities to ensure that planned events actually materialize. Remember, these steps refer to overall organizational control. More specific types of organizational control, like production control, inventory control, or even digital dimensioning control, are based on these same three steps.

These broad controlling steps relate to one another. When performance measurements differ significantly from standard or planned results, managers take corrective action to ensure that planned results actually occur. On the other hand, when performance matches planned results, corrective action is generally not necessary and work continues without modification.

Digital Dimensioning Control

As mentioned at the beginning of this chapter, digital dimensioning control is a special type of organizational control. In reality, understanding organizational control as discussed above is a catalyst for understanding digital dimensioning control. The following sections define and describe the overall purpose of digital dimensioning control.

Defining Digital Dimensioning Control

Digital dimensioning control is a special type of organizational control that focuses on monitoring and evaluating the digital dimensioning process to make sure that expected digital results are achieved. In essence, digital dimensioning control ensures that all planned digital dimensioning results actually materialize. Some managers make the mistake of viewing dimensioning control as a mechanical process. The process is actually very challenging and intricate, and relies on management insight and sound judgment.

To illustrate digital dimensioning control, consider the recent history of OurBeginning.com Inc., an online specialty stationery retailer headquartered in Orlando, Florida.[3] The Orlando company became an overnight sensation in 2000 by running Super Bowl commercials featuring angry brides. At that time, the company seemed to view instant notoriety through multimillion-dollar Super Bowl ads as the primary mechanism for deriving profits from digital activities. Almost a year after the Super Bowl ads, however, the company hadn't turned a profit.

Michael Budowski, OurBeginning.com company president, has recently taken several steps to control digital dimensioning in his company. He is modifying his original plan to make the company more of a stationery wholesaler by selling wedding invitations to bridal and department stores rather than directly to consumers. The company will also scale back its Web site to de-emphasize items like birth announcements and greeting cards. In the future, the company plans to sell only 20 percent of its products directly to consumers, the market it focused on in its Super Bowl commercials.

Budowski's recent steps are based upon management insight and judgment, and focus on ensuring that digital dimensioning in his company actually produces a profit. As with any company, however, digital dimensioning control at OurBeginning.com is a never-ending process. Budowski must continually monitor and, if necessary, improve digital dimensioning activities to ensure that the activities yield expected profit.

The Purpose of Digital Dimensioning Control

Arguably, the most fundamental purpose of controlling digital dimensioning is to assist managers in achieving organizational goals. Managers monitor and improve the digital dimensioning process to maximize positive impact on organizational goal attainment. In sum, the digital dimensioning process entails assessing the organization's digital environment, establishing the organization's digital direction, formulating an action plan that will lead to reaching digital support goals, and subsequently implementing this action plan. Controlling digital dimensioning provides feedback that is critical for determining whether all the steps of the digital dimensioning process are appropriate, compatible, and operating properly.

Digital Dimensioning Control: The Process

Managers take three distinct but related steps to control digital dimensioning in organizations. Naturally, the steps are closely related to the steps for the more general organizational control presented earlier. Specifically, the steps are (1) measure digital performance, (2) compare digital performance with digital standards, and (3) improve digital activities, if necessary, to make sure that digital dimensioning results materialize as planned.

Step 1: Measure Digital Performance

Before managers can plan actions to improve digital dimensioning, they must measure current digital performance. This measurement can be thought of as a *digital audit*, an examination of an organization's digital dimensioning activities. Such an audit may be very comprehensive, emphasizing every facet of a digital dimensioning process, or more narrowly focused, emphasizing only a single part of the process, like enlisting digital expertise. The digital audit can be quite formal, following strict internal procedures, or quite informal, allowing managers self-direction in deciding what digital dimensioning activities to measure and how to measure them. Whether comprehensive or narrow, formal or informal, a digital audit should focus on those issues most likely to gauge what the central thrust of digital dimensioning in an organization is and how to improve it.

No single technique is best for measuring the impact of digital dimensioning activities in all organizations. A number of such measurement techniques exist and can be used. Commonly used digital audit measurement techniques include critical question measurement, surveys measurement, cost-benefit measurement, and third-party measurement. Each of these techniques measures digital performance somewhat differently and affords managers somewhat different data for gauging the effectiveness of digital activity. Each technique is expanded upon below.

Critical Question Measurement *Critical question measurement* is a digital audit measurement technique involving the formulation of important questions regarding the digital dimensioning activities of an organization, the answers to those questions, and the evaluation of those answers. Exact questions to ask vary from organization to organization, depending upon the specifics of an organization's digital dimensioning process. Examples of questions that can be asked are as follows:

Does digital dimensioning have a net positive impact on the organization? "Net" relates to the overall impact of digital dimensioning on the organization. Some digital strategies, for example, might provide an advantage to the organization in one area, but a disadvantage in some other area. For example, Chapter 6 discussed Honeywell's MyPlant.com as a vehicle for Honeywell management to exchange ideas with customers and even sometimes competitors for making operations improvement like reducing overhead or correcting purchasing inefficiencies. While the digital strategy reflected in establishing MyPlant.com might be advantageous in making company operations more efficient and effective, it might also be seriously disadvantageous in providing the same benefit to competitors. In addition, while the digital strategy might be advantageous in giving Honeywell added opportunity to interact with customers, it might also be seriously disadvantageous in providing competitors with access to Honeywell's customers. Each digital dimensioning component must be judged by its total impact on organizational success.

Is digital dimensioning consistent with its digital environment? Digital dimensioning must make sense in light of an organization's digital environment and changes that are likely to occur within it. Is digital strategy, for example, consistent with inevitable new digital technology, changing consumer attitudes about ecommerce, or the supply of labor capable of performing digital dimensioning jobs? Most problems that arise from inconsistencies between digital strategy and digital environment are not the result of a challenge that is too difficult to meet. Instead, such problems normally arise simply because managers fail to invest the time necessary to match digital strategy with the digital environment.

United Parcel Service (UPS) is an example of a company that diligently works to match its digital dimensioning to its digital environment. UPS, the world's largest express carrier and package delivery company, has formidable competitors like Federal Express, DHL, and the U.S. Postal Service. UPS recently made the decision to accelerate its investment in Internet technology, given an assessment of its digital environment.[4] Sensing that ebusiness was definitely the wave of the future, the company made the decision to heighten its focus on building an ebusiness infrastructure as an opportunity to gain a head start on its competitors. As a result, UPS recently launched Document Exchange, a service that speeds documents via the Internet in seconds rather than relying on planes, trains, or delivery vans. With Document Exchange, UPS uses encryption technology that gives customers with Web access a digital fingerprint so that only the sender and receiver know what is sent, who sent it, and when it was sent.

Can organizational resources sustain digital dimensioning? Without appropriate resources, organizations simply cannot make digital dimensioning work. Are the organization's resources sufficient to sustain digital activities? Without enough money, people, materials, or equipment, it is senseless to pursue digital dimensioning activities, no matter how well planned. Digital dimensioning plans must be made while reflecting upon the level of resources an organization can allocate to implementing and sustaining the plans.

Take Garden.com as an example.[5] Garden.com started as a garden products retailer selling goods via the Internet. After a few years of operation, resources were depleted and the company had to shut its doors. In addition to $50 million already raised, the company would have needed between $10 million and $40 million more to remain open. The company had already laid off about 40 percent of its work force and reduced expenses, but it was not sufficient to make Garden.com profitable. Since its founding in 1995, the company's cumulative net loss had grown to $75.5 million. The company was on target to become profitable by early 2002—too little too late. Perhaps if the company's digital dimensioning activities had required less substantial financial resources from the beginning, the company would still be in business today.

Is digital dimensioning too risky? Essentially, risk is the chance of the loss of resources. *Digital dimensioning risk* is the chance of the loss of resources invested in digital dimensioning activities. Some managers invest huge sums of money in digital dimensioning activities, not understanding that the risk of digital dimensioning payoff is low. In such an investment situation, the risk of losing a digital investment, and perhaps an entire organization, is therefore high.

Olive Garden's new digital dimensioning venture, olivegarden.com, provides an excellent illustration of minimizing digital dimensioning risk.[6] Olive Garden, a division of Orlando-based Darden Restaurants, Inc., is a national leader in Italian dining, with 470 restaurants, over 56,000 employees, and $1.6 billion in annual sales. Olivegarden.com was recently launched to assist people in choosing appropriate wine for food they might order when visiting an Olive Garden restaurant. The site includes video illustrating how to open and pour wine and audio explaining how to pronounce wine names.

In assessing the risk of an investment like olivegarden.com, management must consider the cost of digital dimensioning activities. The cost of building and maintaining a site like olivegarden.com can be carefully controlled and requires a relatively modest investment. To recover this investment, management is depending upon visits to olivegarden.com to translate into repeat visits to Olive Garden restaurants, an increase in the amount of wine customers will purchase with their meals, and better overall relationships with customers. The probability of olivegarden.com causing such impact on the Olive Garden restaurant business seems reasonable. As a result, the risk of losing the olivegarden.com investment seems low. Even if olivegarden.com resulted in complete failure, the likelihood of Olive Garden restaurants failing as a result is virtually nonexistent. Overall, the digital dimensioning risk relating to both the investment in the Web site and the continuing viability of Olive Garden restaurants seems negligible.

Survey Measurement *Survey measurement* is a digital audit method for measuring digital performance through the design and administration of specially focused surveys. Such surveys can focus on virtually any facet of the digital dimensioning process, involve people both inside and outside the organization, and be specially designed to suit the individual digital needs of an organization.

Individuals surveyed normally include various company *stakeholders*, people who are interested in an organization because they are significantly affected by the organization's success or failure. Major stakeholders that could be included in digital effectiveness surveying are:

Stockholders.   People interested in the value an organization's stock and related dividends

Employees.   People interested in an organization's wage rates and benefit packages

Creditors.   People interested in the organization's ability to pay its debts

Suppliers.   People interested in retaining the organization as a customer

Government units.   People who see organizations as taxpayers contributing to the costs of running a society

Social interest groups.   People like environmentalists who are interested in an organization's impact on the overall welfare of society

Customers.   People interested in the goods or services produced by an organization

As an example of survey measurement, consider an instrument focusing on an organization's intranet, a component of digital dimensioning that is commonly evaluated through surveys. The purpose of many such intranet surveys is to gather user feedback regarding intranet issues like usage, functionality, and effectiveness of the intranet. Through such a survey, intranet users can share their perceptions about intranet components like corporate information, product information, customer information, and real-time chat capability.

Partial results of an actual intranet survey appear with a disguised company name in Figure 8.1. This particular survey asked intranet users to rate many different areas of intranet content on the amount of information they need from the intranet to do their jobs versus the amount they actually get from the intranet. Five information areas are displayed: quality improvement initiatives, team building, accounting and finance, financial systems, and human resources. According to survey results, in order to do their jobs properly, intranet users believe that they need more job-related information from the intranet in each information area surveyed.

The above example of survey measurement focuses on only one facet of an organization's digital activities, the intranet. In reality, surveying can focus on any digital dimensioning activity. Managers should

Figure 8.1 Intranet user ratings of how much information is received from the Intranet versus how much is needed in five critical information areas.

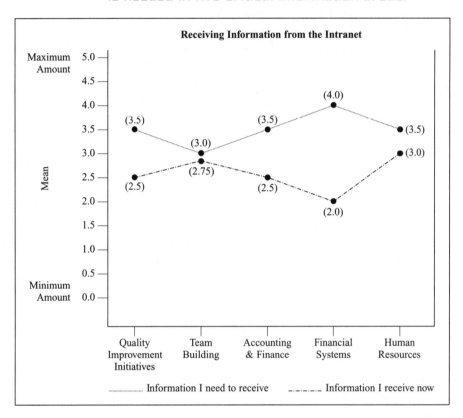

take great care to survey those digital dimensioning activities that are most crucial to digital dimensioning success, and measure their operation validly and reliably.

Cost-Benefit Measurement Cost-benefit is the process of comparing the cost of an activity with the benefits or return of performing the activity. Managers can apply cost-benefit analysis to digital dimensioning activities in organizations. In using cost-benefit analysis to evaluate digital dimensioning, the costs of digital dimensioning activities are isolated to the extent possible. Such costs commonly include the purchase of equipment and software necessary for digital thrust; labor costs regarding planning, design, and implementation of digital dimensioning activities; hosting costs; and main-tenance costs.

Once managers have an accurate profile of digital dimensioning costs, they should summarize the benefits that digital dimensioning provides the organization. Benefits can include issues like revenue both directly and indirectly attributable to digital dimensioning, differential advantage of products gained through digital dimensioning, and lower operational costs resulting from digital dimensioning applications. Managers should keep in mind that these benefits can be measured in both monetary and nonmonetary terms. Monetary terms might include higher revenue, higher profits, or lower operational costs due to digital dimensioning applications. Nonmonetary terms might include higher employee morale due to more shared information, more effective post-purchase customer service, or improved decision making.

Naturally, the overall purpose of cost-benefit analysis is to compare the cost of performing individual digital dimensioning activities against the gain that accrues to the organization as a result of performing the activities. If the gain of performing a digital dimensioning activity is higher than the cost of performing it, management would normally continue performing the activity and look for ways to improve the gain. If the cost is higher than the gain, management would normally discontinue the activity, or look for ways to improve the activity so that the benefit of performing the activity exceeds the cost.

Third-Party Measurement   Managers should keep in mind that third parties are often available that can help in measuring the effectiveness of digital dimensioning activities. One such organization, whose mission is to rate various Web sites and make findings available to consumers and managers, is Gomez, located at Gomez.com. Gomez describes itself as an Internet quality measurement firm. Gomez evaluates Web sites by using the following criteria:

1. ***Ease of use.***   Web sites are judged to be easier to use the more they incorporate features like clear functionality, simplicity in opening an account and purchasing a product, and consistency of design and navigation methods.

2. ***Customer confidence.***   Web sites are judged to build customer confidence the more they are characterized by issues like high reliability, access to knowledgeable customer service representatives, and a secure operating environment.

3. *On-site resources.* Web sites are judged to be rich in on-site resources when they offer a wide range of products and services, provide complete information about the products and services, and offer a full range of ebusiness transactions and information look-up for those products and services.

4. *Relationship services.* Web sites are judged to provide relationship services the more they are characterized by applications aimed at building electronic relationships with site visitors. Electronic relationships are built through site tactics such as allowing visitors to personalize a site or receive frequent buyer rewards. A site that allows visitors to reuse customer data to facilitate future transactions is also a vehicle for building electronic relationships.

5. *Customer cost.* Web sites are judged based upon overall value provided to customers. Web site cost assessments for consumers are based upon the projected total cost of purchasing a typical unit of goods or services for various types of customers. Costs studied can include variables such as comparative cost of products, shipping charges, and handling charges.

Step 2: Compare Digital Performance with Digital Standards

After managers have taken step 1 of the process of controlling digital dimensioning, measuring digital performance, they are ready to take step 2, comparing digital performance with digital standards. *Digital standards* are, simply, acceptable levels of digital results that reflect digital support goals and serve as yardsticks for evaluating digital performance. The specific standards that companies actually establish vary from firm to firm. As a rule, managers should develop standards in all areas corresponding to digital support goals.

For an example illustrating how organizational goals, digital support goals, and digital standards logically relate to one another, refer to Table 8.1. According to this table, an organizational goal to increase profits could have a digital support goal of establishing an intranet to afford salespeople real-time knowledge of the number of high-margin versus low-margin products that are available for sale. In essence, this inventory information can help salespeople to increase company profits by focusing on the sale of higher-margin products when available in inventory. As a related digital standard, the rate of sale of higher-mar-

Table 8.1   Logical relationships among three example goals and related digital support goals and digital standards.

Organizational Goal	Digital Support Goal	Digital Standard
Increase profits	Establish intranet to afford salespeople real-time knowledge about the number of high-margin versus lower-margin products available for sale	The rate of sale of higher-margin products when lower-margin products are also available increases by 20%
Improve customer service	Establish chat capability on corporate Web site to allow customer access to company product experts 24 hours a day, 7 days a week	The majority of customer inquiries are handled to the satisfaction of the customer during a single chat session
Increase products manufactured relative to resources needed to manufacture the products	Establish extranet to enhance timing of resource purchases from key suppliers	Time between the payment for materials and the use of those materials in the products is reduced by 50%

gin products when lower-margin products are also available for sale should increase.

Overall, managers establish organizational goals in critical goal areas. Digital support goals are established to facilitate the accomplishment of those goals, and digital standards are established to set acceptable levels of digital performance so that the digital support goals will be attained. Stated differently, when digital standards are met, then digital support goals are reached, and digital dimensioning contributes to the attainment of organizational goals.

Step 3: Improve Digital Activities

After managers have taken step 1 of the process for controlling digital dimensioning, collecting measurements of digital activity, as well as step 2, comparing the measurements with established digital standards, they are ready to take step 3, improving the effectiveness of digital activities if warranted. *Improving digital activities* is defined as modifying digital dimensioning activities to ensure that they better meet digital standards and thereby better contribute to reaching digital support goals. Improving digital activities may be as simple as changing features on a company Web site or as complicated as reformulating digital strategy.

Figure 8.2 summarizes the main steps of the digital dimensioning control process. Digital dimensioning control begins by measuring digital performance and continues by comparing such measurements with digital standards. Based upon this comparison, a conclusion is made that digital performance either does or does not meet digital standards. If digital performance does meet digital standards, digital improvements are probably not necessary and the measured digital activity continues. On the other hand, if digital performance does not meet digital standards, digital improvements probably should be made, and then the improved digital activity can begin.

Figure 8.2 Major steps for controlling digital dimensioning.

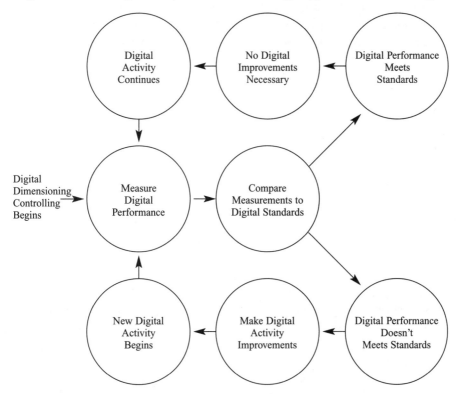

Broadly speaking, digital dimensioning control is aimed at improving the effectiveness of an organization's digital thrust by focusing on improving the digital dimensioning process. Of course, this analysis could include improving the digital dimensioning control process itself by taking steps like enhancing the methods and timeliness of making digital activity measurements. In most situations, corrective action is not necessary if the organization is reaching its digital standards and related digital support goals. Even in this situation, however, management should be very careful. Digital support standards and goals may have been set too low. As a result, corrective action should probably focus on making them more challenging.

Types of Digital Dimensioning Control

Managers have three basic types of digital dimensioning control available to them. These are before-control, during-control, and after-control. The terms *before*, *during*, and *after* all relate to when digital activities are being performed. The type known as "before-control" is digital dimensioning control that takes place prior to the performance of digital activities, whereas the types known as "during-control" and "after-control," respectively, take place during and after the performance of digital activities. Each type is discussed below more fully.

Before-Control

Before-control is digital dimensioning control that takes place before digital activities are performed. In before-control, managers create policies, procedures, and rules aimed at eliminating dysfunctional impact on digital dimensioning proactively. For example, management may believe that a certain level of ebusiness expertise is desirable in all middle-level managers. Using this belief as a basis for before-control, management might establish a policy of hiring middle-level managers or promoting lower-level managers to middle-level positions only if they have this desired level of ebusiness expertise. Through such a policy, management is attempting to eliminate a dysfunctional impact on digital dimensioning before the impact has the opportunity to materialize.

During-Control

During-control is digital dimensioning control that takes place while digital dimensioning activities are being performed. In during-control, managers measure digital activity performance at the time the activities are being performed, compare that measurement against digital standards, and then correct any digital dimensioning activities that are below standard.

One of the most interesting examples of during-control involves General Electric.[7] In the past, management at General Electric was only concerned with keeping the company's core applications—mostly on mainframe computers—constantly functioning. Today, all digital activities are considered mission critical, all the way down to email and Web access. To ensure that people throughout General Electric constantly have email and Web access, servers are continually monitored to make sure that they are working. Whenever any server goes down that would impinge on somebody's ability to conduct business, a siren goes off. The siren immediately alerts management that the server must be brought back online as quickly as possible. Without such during-control, servers at General Electric could be down for more extended time periods causing the company countless dollars in lost business.

After-Control

After-control is digital dimensioning control that takes place after digital dimensioning activities are performed. In after-control, managers measure digital dimensioning activities *after* they are performed, compare the measurements against digital dimensioning standards, and then correct those digital dimensioning activities below standard.

One of the best examples of after-control involves Toys "R" Us.[8] In 1999, as perhaps the world's best-known toy retailer, Toys "R" Us initiated an online shopping venture designed to take advantage of the Christmas buying season. The online venture was a natural extension of the company's traditional toy stores, and seemed like a slam-dunk. Instead, the Web-based venture turned out to be a disaster. Toysrus.com experienced technology breakdowns and delivery logjams that prevented purchased toys from being delivered to children in time for Christmas. Children were disappointed. Parents were irate.

In reflecting on the disastrous digital dimensioning activities of the past, Toys "R" Us is now going back to the Net, but based upon a new deal with Amazon.com, arguably the Internet's largest retailer. The new deal is essentially a new Internet strategy that allows each company to concentrate on what it does best. Toys "R" Us will select the goods for sale, and Amazon will deliver the goods. Toysrus.com CEO John Barbour wouldn't say that the deal with Amazon was a necessity, but agreed that it would make his company a much stronger online competitor.

As this section ends, keep in mind that, in general, managers should not struggle to decide which one type of digital dimensioning control to use in an organization. Instead, managers should strive to institute the best combination of the three types in an organization. In most organizations, managers can make good use of all three types.

Digital Control Hints from Failed Dotcoms

A recent flurry of dotcom failures has provided managers with many insights about what to look for when controlling digital dimensioning activities in organizations.[9] Although these insights are most closely related to more pure dotcom ventures, they can also apply to more traditional organizations with added digital thrust—click-and-mortar companies. In controlling digital dimensioning, managers should:

Ensure that digital activities are based on a sound revenue, cost, and profit model.   Many failed dotcoms were based upon business models that didn't generate enough revenues and were saddled with initial high costs that made initial success impossible. Managers should monitor the business models upon which digital thrusts are based and, if necessary, make changes to ensure that revenue, costs, and profits are at acceptable levels.

Ensure that digital activities provide differential advantage. Many failed dotcoms provided goods or services that were much like those of competitors. Managers should evaluate their digital thrust against the differential advantage that it provides and, if necessary, make changes to ensure that the competitive advantage of digital thrust is maximized.

Ensure that products are sold above cost.   Although this might seem obvious, many failed dotcoms operated under the assumption that selling products below cost is an effective strategy for gaining customers. Although this assumption may gain customers, if the strategy of selling below cost is maintained, failure of the organization is inevitable. A case in point is pets.com. Selling products below cost is often cited as the primary reason that it had to be shut down. For pets.com, delivery costs were a primary problem. Shipping products like an 18-pound bag of cat food was very expensive. Some at pets.com believed that patience would have yielded mechanisms to ensure breakeven and eventually profitability. Getting beyond the harm caused by selling below cost, however, proved to be too much of an obstacle to overcome.

Ensure that advertising expenditures are thoughtfully made. Many failed dotcoms seemed to believe there was no limit to what management could spend on advertising. This belief seemed based on the assumption that the more that management spends on advertising, the more successful the company will be. Boo.com, an Internet fashion retailer, was recently sold and relaunched under new management.[10] Many believe that overly aggressive advertising expenditures severely weakened the original company. Originally, Boo.com spent a whopping $223 million in advertising and promotions, including a $42 million print and TV launch program. Overall, the company got a very meager return on the enormous advertising dollars spent in hopes of generating significant numbers of customers and profit dollars.

Ensure that economic cycles are thoughtfully considered. Some failed dotcoms seemed to believe that Internet-based companies are insulated from economic cycles. Mortgage.com started as a company that provided home mortgages over the Internet. During its early history, interest rates were falling and people rushed to the Internet to find the best possible refinancing for their home mortgages. When interest rates began moving up, however, people seemed much less attracted to originating mortgages on the Internet. As a result, Mortgage.com saw its customer traffic dwindle significantly. Even after attempts to refocus the company to gain added origination mortgage business, the company simply had to cease operation.

Back to Procter & Gamble

This section illustrates how digital dimensioning principles apply to real organizations. Consider the following information as digital dimensioning advice that an ebusiness consultant might have given Procter & Gamble management as input for performing its digital activities. To gain maximum benefit from this section, explore pg.com before reading further.

"Your plans to revitalize company performance through innovation and product improvement are certainly admirable. Organization 2005's goal of making your culture more Internet-savvy is certainly in line with the times. Establishing digitally based collaborative online technology, business-to-consumer ecommerce systems, and online communication systems with suppliers can all be very instrumental in establishing Procter & Gamble's future success.

"Your digital dimensioning plans are commendable. Remember, however, that such plans will only be helpful to your company if management is able to control digital dimensioning. Digital dimensioning control is a special type of organizational control that focuses on monitoring and evaluating the digital dimensioning process at P&G to make sure that your expected digital results are indeed achieved.

"How do you make sure that expected digital results are achieved? Start by measuring digital performance. Assume, for example, that you're starting to build your new online communication system with suppliers. You can measure such issues as how the development of the application is proceeding and working from a technical as well as from a business viewpoint. You can do this by using critical question measurements, survey measurements, cost-benefit measurements, or perhaps even third-party measurements. Each of these different measurement techniques will give you a somewhat different picture of how the new digital communication system is progressing or operating.

"Once you have taken measurements regarding the initiation and operation of your new digital communication system with suppliers, compare measurements with what you expected to see as a result of establishing the new system. Based upon this comparison, take steps to improve the new system if necessary.

"When controlling this new digital system, you'll probably be able to use before-control, during-control, and after-control. Use before-control to create policies that will help ensure the success of the new application. One such policy might be that new equipment purchased by both P&G and suppliers to build the system will be purchased from the same vendor in order to ensure equipment compatibility. Use during-control to assess how the system is working as it operates. For example, traffic patterns and even message contents can be monitored constantly to make sure that appropriate company-supplier relationships are being established. Use after-control to evaluate the new system after some time period of use. Historical data for the time period, perhaps quarterly data, can be used to assess effectiveness and efficiency of the new system. Naturally, system improvements can be made based upon conclusions derived from historical data. Make sure that you do not wait too long to view this historical perspective. Digital issues move quickly, and waiting too long to make system improvements might prove fatal.

"You can learn much about how to control your new digital thrust by examining the mistakes many of the failed dotcoms made. First, be sure that all your digital activities are based upon a sound revenue, cost, and profit model. Remember, failed dotcoms are not Internet failures, but business failures. Make sure that your digital activities are based upon a sound business model. Second, build your digital activities so that they provide some type of differential advantage for the company. Perhaps Organization 2005 will allow P&G to cut operating costs or allow customers to be uniquely introduced to P&G products. As another example of what can be learned from the failed dotcoms, make sure that products are offered at above-cost prices. A number of failed dotcoms seemed to focus on buying market share by selling products below cost. These companies seemed to believe that they would subsequently make up the loss and find significant profits after significant market share was gained. But the significant profits never came."

Digital Dimensioning Resolutions

- Make sure that everyone in your organization understands the meaning of *controlling digital dimensioning.*

- Keep emphasizing the purpose of digital dimensioning control.

- When appropriate, use critical questions to measure digital performance.

- When appropriate, use surveys to measure digital performance.

- When appropriate, use cost-benefit analysis to evaluate the worth of performing digital activities.

- When appropriate, use third-party ratings to measure digital performance.

- Compare the measurements of digital activities with established digital standards.

- Make sure that digital support goals and digital standards are logically consistent.

- Use before-control, during-control, and after-control to make sure that digital activities are managed appropriately.

chapter 9

New-Economy Culture: The Key to Digital Dimensioning Success

Executive Preview

This chapter describes the unique attributes of corporate culture in the new economy and its importance in the digital dimensioning process. The chapter's primary premise focuses upon management's need to create a culture appropriate for ebusiness success. The chapter opens by describing the cultural characteristics of Hewlett-Packard, Inc., a designer and manufacturer of computing devices and peripherals and provider of ebusiness-related services to consumers and institutions. A general overview of the role of culture follows, with an emphasis on the important part that culture plays in organizations and society as the mortar between people. The chapter then presents a description of corporate culture, its function within the organization, and its importance as a management indicator. Next, the chapter outlines the new considerations of corporate culture, as some have changed significantly from those in the old economy. What follows is a practical guide for managers in the process of building and refining their culture for operation in the new economy. The "Back to Hewlett-Packard" section contains advice and suggestions a consultant could have given company management in building its culture for the new economy. The chapter ends with a list of resolutions that are practical steps you can adopt to build and refine the corporate culture in your organization with respect to digital dimensioning premises.

Spotlight

Hewlett-Packard, Inc., Focuses on Culture Development to Accelerate into the New Economy[1]

Hewlett-Packard, Inc. (HP), a designer and manufacturer of computing devices and peripherals, provides a host of ebusiness services to institutions around the world. Founded in 1939 by William Hewlett and David Packard, HP has developed an outstanding reputation for technology leadership and innovation over its six decades of existence. Given its storied history and long-standing tradition, the coming of Internet technology and ebusiness advances presented HP with both opportunities and threats. Some argued that HP was moving too slowly and that its competitive advantages were being compromised.

To navigate the precarious waters, HP named Carly Fiorina, an experienced corporate executive, its CEO in July 1999. Perhaps her greatest challenge lay in guiding the company's 84,000 employees toward the tremendous market share and cost-saving opportunities that the Internet presented to HP. The tall order involved reinventing how HP was marketed, how it developed new products, and how it operated internally and externally.

While the challenge before Ms. Fiorina involved a host of new strategies and tasks, her first priority centered on the development and refinement of HP's corporate culture. Fiorina sought to propel the large company into the Internet age by eliminating politics and bureaucracy, and by rewarding risk taking and "radical ideas." Twelve months later, the company had a new advertising campaign, a host of new ebusiness offerings, and a revamped culture designed to retain employees, stimulate a "balanced" work life for team members, and cast a healthy focus on ebusiness.

Understanding New-Economy Culture

What's Ahead? The Spotlight described the unique cultural circumstances of Hewlett-Packard and serves as a testament to the importance of culture as a management consideration in the new economy. This chapter focuses on individual aspects of corporate culture and offers insight into those characteristics unique to the new economy. The following sections will provide both an understanding of such considerations and practical steps toward effective implementation in any organization.

Introduction

Previous chapters have examined the components and framework of the digital dimensioning process. From issues of personnel and strategy to those of implementation and evaluation, this book has described how managers can reach the organization's goals and objectives through the creation and implementation of digital applications. The final consideration for managers involves creating the appropriate internal climate for implementing the digital dimensioning process throughout the organization. This internal climate—corporate culture—is critical with respect to effective digital dimensioning because it serves as the enabler of the entire process. In reality, no business strategy can or will succeed without the right culture in place.[2]

This chapter addresses the important area of organizational culture and describes the role it plays in an organization's success. The chapter will outline the dynamics of cultural systems outside of organizations in an effort to provide insight into the way people live and work together. Then the chapter will shift its focus to the culture within organizations and draw parallels with noncorporate communities. An overview of new-economy cultural considerations will also be provided to help managers grasp the concerns of contemporary workplace norms. Just as they must keep up with technology, managers must stay abreast of the latest workplace culture developments as a means of maintaining and increasing organizational competitiveness. Finally, the chapter will explore the cultural considerations of the digital dimensioning process and present practical steps for building a strong culture that fosters organizational success.

The most fundamental cultural consideration of the digital dimensioning process is that it involves change and innovation within an organization. More specifically, the process indeed *demands* both. For an organization to endure evolution, employees must both be receptive to and participate in change. While openness to new ideas does vary from one employee to another, change—whether positive or negative—is most often a factor of the culture that unites the people therein. If an organization is not poised for change and innovation, management must alter the culture so that the organization will accommodate the new ideas inherent in the digital dimensioning process. The burden for organizational change rests upon the shoulders of management and then upon the rest of the organization. Ensuring that the transition occurs is a function of leadership and will be addressed later in the chapter.

Understanding that digital dimensioning success necessitates the presence of the proper culture, managers must strive to create it within their organizations prior to and concurrent with the first steps of the digital dimensioning process. To thoroughly understand the practical steps that managers can take in doing so, they must first understand the nature of culture as a function of people systems in general. A *people system* is a broad generalization of formal and informal groups of people living, working, or operating together. Examples of people systems range from families and social groups to churches and military divisions. An understanding of corporate culture begins with an understanding of how culture holds people together, dictates their behavior, and determines the fate of new ideas and conventions in societies and communities. Once this baseline understanding is achieved, the implications of culture within corporations are much clearer and the steps that managers must take to build a healthy culture are much more certain.

Culture: The Mortar of People Systems

Culture is by no means a new concept. After all, it has been present as an intangible factor within groups since people first started cooperating and living together, just beyond the dawn of human civilization. Whenever people live or work together, culture naturally develops as a defining element of their coexistence. Culture is a relatively intangible element that serves as a mortarlike bond between those in any people system, whether that system comprises a native tribe in South America, a civic community in a Midwestern farm town, or a start-up corporation in Silicon Valley. *Culture* is simply the contemporary label for the natural bond between people that guides how they talk, work, dress, celebrate, and perform any other activity that might be relevant to their existence. In the end, this bond connects and unites individuals and becomes the mortar that holds them together.

Individual cultures are characterized by a number of variables that make them unique. These variables include language, belief systems, and rituals and together establish patterns of acceptable behavior among members of a culture.

Language

The first variable, language, simply refers to the vocabulary, tone, and dialect of any group of people. Language is at the heart of communication and is designed both to share messages among those intended to understand them and to veil messages from those not intended to. Overall, language varies throughout geographic regions and develops naturally through shared experiences among different groups. Oftentimes, groups of people will essentially speak the same language but develop or use variations of it according to environment or experiences. Many people in the United States, for example, speak English. However, the vocabulary, dialect, and tone may vary significantly among inner cities, rural areas, and suburbs. Even though they might all speak the English language, individuals living in a Midwestern farm town might have a very different manner of speaking than do people living in a neighborhood in Brooklyn. Those individual language patterns tend to become strong elements of commonality among the various groups and create identity for the group members.

Belief Systems

A shared system of beliefs is a second element of culture that is highly important and determinate of its individuality. Since the beginning of time, civilizations have sought to explain the unexplainable through scientific and religious rationale. For example, before the development of contemporary meteorology and astronomy, different groups believed weather and seasonal patterns were caused by what we now consider myths and folklore. Beliefs like these become the foundation for the explanation of the trivial and for the rationale of the profound. Many groups are so deeply rooted in their beliefs that they view the beliefs of others as potential threats to their own.

Values often stem from beliefs. Cultures begin to place various levels of emphasis on different beliefs that become values. These beliefs and values begin to serve as targets toward which a culture's conscious and subconscious actions are directed. And people within different cultures tend to exhibit behavior that is consistent with these values and beliefs. The Hindu culture, for example, holds the cow in the most sacred regard. Hindus go to great lengths to both protect and honor cows. Relationships within a culture tend to strengthen as the consistency of behavior with shared values increases. For this reason, values and beliefs are at the heart of cultural strength. In fact, this is why differences in values and beliefs are often at the heart of political strife and even wars.

Rituals

A third variable of culture is ritual. People within a culture identify with the repetition of rituals and customs indigenous to it. They create and repeat various rituals and ceremonies to commemorate occasions, memorialize events or people, or celebrate important occurrences. These ceremonies are often at the heart of a culture's shared memory and are created and repeated to reinforce its values and beliefs. Cultures have varying ways in which they perform their rituals. Birth and death rituals, for example, are handled very differently among cultures.

Why Is Culture Important?

The variables of language, beliefs, and rituals all combine to synthesize culture. Variances in each determine cultural identity and individuality. But why are these factors so important? Why is there an entire academic discipline—social anthropology—devoted to these issues? Quite simply, the idea of culture is important because it helps to decode the perspective, actions, and behavior patterns of those within various groups of people. Leaders strive to understand and anticipate the needs of their people based upon their cultural tendencies. Cultures seek to decode the mysteries of the behavior of other cultures for the purposes of economic and social cooperation. Cultural differences are often center stage during global conferences, peace negotiations, and wars. Without an understanding of how cultures might potentially co-exist or clash, leaders are at a disadvantage.

Cultural understanding is certainly critical when corporations attempt to do business in foreign countries. Many corporations train their employees to be aware of and sensitive to foreign rituals and beliefs because of their importance in negotiations and other business dealings. An American fast-food restaurant chain that serves beef hamburgers in America must realize that predominantly Hindu cultures like India will most likely be unreceptive to many of its products. In addition, advertisers must be cautious of using words in foreign countries whose languages might translate them in a negative way. Such scenarios show that a lack of cultural sensitivity or consideration can be very embarrassing and costly to corporations.

Cultural study among people systems is critical for these practical reasons. Essentially, though, the variables of people systems—language, beliefs, and rituals—help decode and predict the behavior of individuals and their collective people systems. Cultural understanding helps in projecting the acceptance of new thoughts or ideas by those within a people system. Understanding rituals gives insight into choosing the appropriate times to influence individuals within a culture. Many parents in America, for example, have particularly strong influence over their small children in November and December, who know that Santa Claus's naughty and nice checklist plays a very important role. This is a particularly great time to ask children to clean their rooms because they tend to be very open to such ideas during the holiday ritual.

The most important thing to understand and appreciate about culture is the bonding properties that it possesses. Culture is the mortar between various individuals within a system. It has implications for what people say, what they do, and what they value and believe in. When managers understand how this bonding property works between individuals in noncorporate communities, they can appreciate and consider the parallel implications within corporate organizations.

Corporate Culture: The Organizational People System

Like individual societies in various regions, organizations are people systems too. Fundamental differences do exist, but the high level of cooperation and collaboration creates the same dynamics of communities. Similar to communities, cultures within corporations embody the variables of language, belief systems, and rituals. In addition, culture plays a critical part in many areas of the organization such as customer service, human resources, and quality assurance. Understandably, these variables can have a direct impact on sales and profitability. Cultural understanding among organizations is critical in evaluating vendors, planning acquisitions, and implementing new strategies. Additionally, the suitability of these factors plays a key role in the digital dimensioning process and the success of the organization as a whole. Organizations like Hewlett-Packard must be mindful of the cultural issues present within their operations and adjust them as needed.

Language in Organizations

Like societies, companies develop their own languages and dialects based upon shared experience or knowledge. Team members at Darden Restaurants call the Red Lobster Create Your Own Platter menu item "CYOP," for short. While most customers would never recognize this naming convention, company employees use it among themselves for purposes of brevity. Software companies speak in jargon according to the proprietary nature or privacy of their assets. Prior to its public launch in 1995, Windows 95 was referred to by Microsoft insiders as "Project Chicago" to hide its true identity. Similar to ethnic enclaves, companies naturally develop shared languages that help to bond employees together and separate "insiders" from "outsiders." Language can indeed be a significant variable among corporate cultures.

Belief Systems in Organizations

In addition to language, many companies have very strong belief systems at the foundation of their cultures. Whether a company rests upon a mission statement, purpose statement, management credo, company vision, or some combination of them all, employees look to shared values to direct behavior. Some companies, like Southwest Airlines, believe that work should be fun. As a result, employees wear festive attire, make jokes during safety announcements, and sing songs to customers throughout the flight. Priority Associates, a faith-based organization promoting spirituality in the workplace, believes that workers today are in dire need of balance, focus, and direction in their everyday lives. These values are at the heart of their national meetings, omnipresent in their speeches and workshops, and printed on roadside billboards, coffee cups, and literature. What's more, every member of the Priority Associates team falls back on these values on an everyday basis. While views that oppose Southwest and Priority certainly exist, both organizations feed off customers and partners who share theirs. Understanding their values helps to distinguish between likely sources of assistance and resistance. By continuing to emphasize and reinforce an organization's values, managers are able to strengthen the bonds between employees.

Rituals in Organizations

Building on the notion of belief systems and values, organizations often create and repeat rituals designed to reinforce them. *Ritual* is a word that conjures up images of abstract and spiritual practices. In terms of corporate culture, though, rituals can be very simple devices used to reinforce history or values. Some companies have enthusiastic celebrations after monumental events like contract signings or project completions. Team members at ScreamingMedia.com, a business-to-business provider of online content, clap loudly after a sales executive closes a sale and beats on a bongo drum in front of the entire company. Others throw parties for new employees as a way to make a new person feel a sense of belonging. Whatever the case, rituals create a shared sense of "how things are done" by virtue of their ongoing repetition.

The Importance of Culture in Organizations

Language, beliefs, and rituals serve as critical factors in building corporate cultures. Most importantly, these factors are instruments of organizational unity and solidarity. Especially during times when adverse circumstances can threaten an organization's survival, corporate culture becomes the bonding element that holds people together. Culture is about sustainability.[3]

Understanding the nature of each variable within an organization is key to decoding its cultural identity. It is also important to note that one or more of these variables can have negative or positive effects on a culture. For example, some companies do not have clearly articulated or collectively accepted beliefs. When beliefs are either fragmented or nonexistent, the actions of organizational members can be inconsistent or counterproductive. If one manager of an organization believes in social responsibility and another does not, the potential for hostility or inconsistent company action exists. A lack of consensual values results in an organization that lacks the bonding effects that belief consistency maintains and reinforces. Managers must examine the nature of these variables within organizations as an indicator of the positive and negative aspects of a culture.

The same can be said for various corporations that have individual cultures all their own. Cultural difference is often a pivotal factor that is carefully analyzed prior to mergers and acquisitions. Those evaluating the proposed merger between America Online, a company with a very contemporary culture, and Time Warner, a company with a very traditional culture, have speculated that cultural differences will create potential problems within the combined company. Only time will tell. As in society, clashes in corporate culture can often lead to disagreement, strife, or even destruction.

In addition to merger possibilities, cultural fits are ideal in client-vendor relationships. When two companies are collaborating and cooperating for indefinite lengths of time, it is vital that their cultural patterns are compatible. If one company's culture views established deadlines as flexible while the other thinks of them as concrete, the potential for project conflict exists.

Just as in civilizations, corporate cultures develop naturally and automatically. There was not a time in history when an innovative manager decided to build the world's first corporate culture. Culture autonomously develops as an unwritten manifesto of "how things are." Managers must understand how culture works and how it evolves in order to influence its direction and ensure its positive effects.

Fundamentals of New-Economy Culture

Culture in corporations has evolved significantly over the years. Contemporary pundits use the terms *old school* and *new school* to describe the changing tone in corporations over the last several decades. The contrast between the two is fundamentally correlative to that between the old and new economy. At one time, the term *corporate America* used to conjure up images of starched white shirts and ties scurrying around sterile office environments. Such characteristics have no doubt been supplanted by a more relaxed atmosphere of casual dress, workplace policies, and office environments. Moreover, employers are searching for ways to make work fun. From elaborate corporate bashes to in-office recreation rooms, employers are injecting enjoyment and meaning into the work lives of their employees and redefining the meaning of work itself. In 1995 IBM, well known for its very formal dress code and workplace policies, overhauled those policies completely to allow casual attire in the office and began construction on a more relaxed headquarters. The announcement, made by Louis V. Gerstner, Jr., was one of the first in a series of steps to modernize the corporate giant's culture.[4] Because of IBM's large presence and established reputation for formal business attire, this was seen as a very serious indicator of a changing climate in the workplace. IBM resounded and amplified the signal that khakis and collared sport shirts in the office were professionally acceptable. It is important for managers to recognize these trends and take steps to maintain a culture that is consistent with culture's widespread evolution.

Beyond just dress, the overall tone in corporations is very different today. Many companies that operated under old-economy standards have made transitions to those of the new economy. Fundamentally, the comfortable and relaxed standards in the new economy are much more attractive to members of the work force. Given the challenge of enlisting and retaining expertise in the new economy, employers are scrambling to make their working environments more accommodating to current and potential team members. Although certainly beneficial and attractive to employees, changes in workplace standards are indeed attractive to employers as well. And while the changes in the new economy workplace are sometimes more costly, those employers who do embrace them are likely to be more successful with recruitment and retention than those who do not.

Employee loyalty was a much different animal than it is today. Many studies show that employee loyalty is tied to job satisfaction, opportunities for personal growth, organizational direction, and recognition of life balance. A 1998 study by AON Consulting generated a Workforce Commitment Index (WCI), a measurement of varying organizational loyalty from year to year. Among several factors, the study found "A Fearless Culture"—the extent to which the organization encourages you to challenge the way things are done—to be the issue of highest correlation to employee loyalty.[5] Such a finding serves as a strong message to management that culture plays a critical role in employee loyalty, the absence of which can be very costly to an organization. Given possible low-unemployment conditions of the new economy, employee loyalty becomes of vital concern. Whereas the old economy placed much of the power with the organization where employees were expendable and replaceable, the new economy places it firmly with the employee where the prospects of replacement are very difficult for and costly to the organization.

Not only were worker loyalties and tendencies quite different in the old economy, but corporate structures were very foreign from the ones commonly found today. Most organizational charts were completely vertical, with a few folks on top giving the orders and the masses underneath standing ready to receive and obey them without question. This old model of rigid hierarchy has been supplanted by much more decentralized systems whereby authority, strategic thinking, and innovation rest with the entire organization—not just the proud few at the top. Organization charts in the new economy are broader, flatter structures designed to include and empower those who were formerly at the bottom.

This shift in hierarchy has been caused in part by a shift in leadership philosophy. The rigid hierarchies of the old economy were led by those who wanted to maintain the vast majority of power and control over organizational decisions. Those at the bottom of the organization chart were simply the ordertakers and "doers." This is no longer the case, as innovative managers of today embody new styles of leadership. Leaders in the new economy look to empower—not squelch—the strategic and creative participation of those in extended areas of the organization. They look not to simply wield the iron fist of control and authority but to support and empower the functions and initiatives of those on the front lines.

Empowerment, the notion of investing power and authority within employees, is sometimes thought of as a flighty, trendy component of the new economy. In its simplest form, though, empowerment has been a baseline workplace concern for decades. Early management theorists have preached the importance of empowering employees through management style. According to the argument, empowering employees is a tactic for enriching jobs and thereby a method for motivating employees and encouraging them to be as productive as possible.

Consistent with the message of early management writers, empowerment plays a key role in defining the new-economy workplace. The empowered employee is not someone who simply takes instructions and follows orders. Instead, the empowered employee participates in the process of determining the organization's direction and formulating the ensuing direction. The television ads run by Monster.com satirize this change in workplace demeanor. The ads feature representatives of the future work force—children—spouting ironic workplace aspirations like "When I grow up, I want to file all day" and "I want to be a yes man. Yes sir, coming sir," to sarcastically highlight the changing tone of today's workplace. The "When I Grow Up" campaign struck such a deep chord with the audience that it yielded a 450 percent increase in job searches within 24 hours of the campaign's launch. *Wired* magazine gave the campaign its Most WIRED TV Spot award for its "clever, creative" approach to technology advertising.[6] Monster has accurately annunciated the notion that the member of today's work force wants to be empowered and enabled, not squelched.

The old guard has certainly shifted to a new one. The tone of business has changed from a rigid, cold one to a flexible, warm one. Things have changed within the corporate culture to reflect the changing needs and desires of workers. As managers embrace digital dimensioning within their organizations, they must be aware of the considerations of culture.

Organizational Culture and the Digital Dimensioning Process

Given an understanding of societal and organizational cultural systems along with some specific considerations of workplace culture in the new economy, managers can begin to explore the nature of building or modifying culture within their own organizations. Many managers tend to focus on the traditional management functions of sales, marketing, operations, and finance without lending significant time to the element of culture building. The digital dimensioning process requires that managers explore this very issue in depth and progressively move toward refining this critical organizational component. As illustrated in Figure 9.1, organizational culture and digital dimensioning activities each have iterative effects on the other. Modifications to organizational culture have impact on the digital dimensioning process. Likewise, digital dimensioning activities have effects upon organizational culture.

Figure 9.1   Digital dimentioning activities and organizational culture have significant impact on one another.

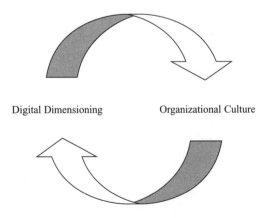

Digital Dimensioning   Organizational Culture

There is no single prescription or blueprint for building an organizational culture. Understandably, the different circumstances of individual organizations require a unique cultural road map for every organization. For example, a start-up company aggressively vying for a "first-mover advantage" in the online consumer marketplace requires a much different culture to succeed than does an established conglomerate seeking to defend a position of market leadership in an industrial manufacturing segment. The former contains very different cultural concerns than does the latter.

Cultural Health

Corporate cultures represent the working environment within organizations. Just as healthy crops are the product of a carefully tended field, an organization's success is the product of healthy working conditions. Like a farmer and his crops, a manager must be mindful of creating the right environment for employees and their work.

A healthy, positive culture represents a working environment where workers are satisfied with their roles, feel a genuine sense of belonging to the organization, and are positively impacted as people by their work experiences. On the contrary, negative cultures have a detrimental impact upon organizational members through the unhealthy conditions that they present. Employees within a negative culture can feel overworked, can feel disconnected from the organization, and are often in search of other employment opportunities. Naturally, the existence of a healthy corporate culture promotes teamwork, company pride, innovation, and creativity. Factors like these contribute to an organization's quest for its objectives and ultimate success. Certainly, negative cultural circumstances can inhibit growth or even promote an organization's erosion.

Corporate cultures are living, breathing entities that are subject to change. Healthy cultures can become sick very quickly. Likewise, negative cultures can be transformed into positive ones through a series of attentive steps. The difference between the two is a primary factor in determining the success or failure of an organization.

However different the cultural issues are across the spectrum, though, any culture is capable of being "healthy" or "unhealthy" in its own regard. A healthy culture is simply defined as an organizational climate that furthers the organization toward its objectives by inherently maximizing the benefits of human resources. Contrarily, an unhealthy culture is one whose very nature inhibits the organization from moving toward its objectives by allowing the negative facets of human resources to flourish.

In order to understand the health of an organization fully, managers must first understand the nature of cultural health in an effort to build it within an existing or forthcoming organization. Like the health of a human being, organizational health can be measured and diagnosed based upon the symptoms it shows. Table 9.1 lists some respective symptoms of healthy and unhealthy cultures. This table highlights a variety of indicators that managers can use to evaluate the health of an organization's culture. While in isolation these factors may not necessarily present an accurate profile of an organization's cultural health taken collectively, these factors should arm managers with valuable information to put together a well-rounded assesssment. Managers must broadly and objectively study their organizational climate by analyzing the issues raised in the table. Overall, these issues will serve as telling indicators of an organization's cultural health. For managers involved in newer organizations whose cultures are just growing and forming, these indicators may serve as micro-objectives in building an organizational culture.

Once managers appreciate the difference between a healthy culture and an unhealthy one, the next area of focus involves improving the

Table 9.1   Symptoms of cultural health.

Healthy Culture	Unhealthy Culture
Low turnover	High turnover
Low absenteeism	High absenteeism
High rate of internal employment referrals	Low rate of internal employment referrals
Strong participation in optional company events	Weak participation in optional company events
Constructive, positive responses to employee opinion surveys	Anger-ridden responses to employee opinion surveys
Willingness of employees to share information with others for the benefit of the company	Tendency of employees to veil information in an effort to promote self over the organization as a whole
Consistent belief systems	Fragmented belief systems
Displays of behavior consistent with the organization's purpose or mission	Displays of behavior contrary to the organization's purpose or mission

health of a culture in an unhealthy state or enhancing the health of an already healthy one. Managers can look to the three variables of culture—language, belief systems, and rituals—to do so.

Language is a very strong indicator of cultural health because it is the baseline component of how individuals communicate. The element of language—utilized in face-to-face meetings, telephone conversations, and email messages—is the encoder of messages between members of a culture. Managers can analyze the nature of employee conversations to determine whether the information therein is open and collaborative or guarded and isolating. From the perspective of diagnosis, managers must observe not only *what* people say to one another but *how* they say it. Are the conversations between most individuals curt, guarded, and veiled, or are they typically open, spirited, and embracing? In healthy cultures, communication is typically more open and inclusive rather than guarded and exclusive.

If managers sense that the element of language is contributing negatively to the culture, they must alter this variable. Managers—from middle management to the CEO—must participate in dialogue with the entire organization to set a positive tone of conversation. This can be achieved through brown-bag lunches where two-way conversation is encouraged or in incidental contact that is programmed by management. John Chambers, CEO of Cisco Systems, wheels around an ice cream cart between employee cubicles and asks employees open-ended questions about how the company can improve and/or be more accommodating to their needs. By allowing and encouraging collaborative discussion at the highest level of the organization, Chambers is setting the tone within the company that such discussion is valuable and useful communication. Managers in the new economy must understand and influence the nature of language within the organization as a key means toward building a healthy organizational culture.

In addition to what people say (and how they say it), it is important to be aware of the beliefs that represent the fundamental purpose of the organization's existence. After all, belief systems are at the core of an individual's existence. In terms of the organization, it is critical that fundamental values and beliefs are consistent across the organization.

The more disjointed and inconsistent the beliefs and values, the greater the likelihood that organizational solidarity and health will be significantly diminished. It is certainly permissible and even encouraged that differences of opinion exist within an organization. But fundamental values of the firm must be consistently and repeatedly adhered to in every possible circumstance. If a firm values corporate responsibility as part of its operating philosophy or direction, everyone in that organization must understand this and embody it. Now it is certainly permissible for organizational members to disagree about how this value is embodied. One employee might argue for the organization's financial sponsorship of AIDS research while another prefers companywide volunteer participation with Habitat for Humanity. While a difference of opinion exists in the vehicle for embodying the value, each employee agrees on the value itself.

If a manager senses that belief systems across the organization are disjointed or inconsistent, he or she must act swiftly to build consistency as soon as possible in an effort to positively influence cultural health. The first step is to clearly annunciate the company's values to everyone in the company. Oftentimes, organizational members are unclear about the organization's stance on various issues. The first step in adoption of values and beliefs is elementary awareness of what those beliefs are. A second step in building belief consistency is in openly praising those who display consistency with those beliefs and directly reprimanding those who display inconsistency with them. Beliefs are not respected unless leadership demands that they be respected. A third step focuses on the fundamental role of leadership itself. Management at all levels must set a positive example of belief adherence with each single action. Michael Eisner, longtime CEO of Disney, exemplifies his firm's value of cleanliness by personally picking up items of trash from the grounds of the company's theme parks. By participating in the most rudimentary of tasks, company leadership can have a profound influence on an organization's belief systems simply through demonstrating their everyday importance within the organization

Once beliefs and values are clearly articulated and embodied across the organization, management's next step is to maintain and sustain their vibrancy. Rituals are tools at the disposal of management designed to build culture and community through the performance and repetition of some commemorative act. Some organizations have very informal rituals like companywide lunches or casual outings. Others have very formal, focused rituals like award ceremonies and banquets designed to commemorate an event or milestone. Many of these rituals—formal or informal—serve as appropriate and unique times to emphasize values. Some rituals are directly correlative to values and should be performed and repeated whenever possible.

Ritual is important to an organization's health because it reinforces values and builds tradition. Both of these outcomes are indeed positive aspects of a culture's health. Managers must take steps to reinforce values whenever possible. Rituals are no doubt an effective way to do so. When analyzing an organization's cultural health, it is vital to examine the state of rituals within. If rituals are nonexistent, take the time to consider what rituals might be appropriate. It can be a very effective cultural-building activity to ask employees what rituals they would find meaningful or to participate in the creation of rituals.

The effects of culture upon organizations are indeed very profound. Managers must be very aware of cultural issues as they move forward with implementing the digital dimensioning process. And frankly, managers must be conscious of cultural considerations throughout each step of the process itself.

Enlisting Digital Expertise   Undoubtedly, the first step in the digital dimensioning process involves enlisting those internal and external specialists to champion various digital activities. When managers proceed with identifying those personnel, they must be very conscious of personal characteristics that go far beyond skill and education. Prospective participants in the digital dimensioning process must be potentially compatible with the organization's existing culture so as not to *disrupt* the internal climate but to *enhance* it. Management can dissect this consideration by evaluating the culture of a candidate's existing employer, exploring the personality of a candidate during an interview, or simply asking the candidate about what type of culture is most suitable to the candidate's optimal performance.

Beyond individual experts, the digital dimensioning process sometimes involves outside contractors like Web development firms and management consulting firms that have individual cultures themselves. Because working engagements with such firms can last several months or even multiple years, it is important that the culture of the contracting organization is consistent with that of the contractor.

A recent example of such a conflict involved Web consultancy iXL, the Atlanta-based provider of ebusiness services to Fortune 500 corporations around the globe. iXL acquired three West Coast firms that had very relaxed dress codes and workplace policies: "All three had cultures different from the corporate professionalism of iXL—. . . staffers were more likely to have mohawks and piercings than tailored suits."[7] Such instances of difference created a "culture clash and a mass exodus" of employees from iXL's West Coast operations.

Analyzing Online Environment and Establishing Digital Direction   Management must also consider cultural issues when analyzing the online environment of the organization. When evaluating the factors both inside and outside the organization that can affect digital tactics, culture becomes a critical role player. Managers need to be aware of the organization's culture when identifying critical factors. Because an analysis of the organization's environment directly precedes the establishment of its digital direction, those participating must individually identify the factors that are either consistent, inconsistent, or impartial with regard to the organization's central values. If part of the analysis reveals a strong opportunity in a particular area of business, digital dimensioning participants must be mindful of the potential reaction and cooperation of people in the organization.

In addition, the digital support grid calls management to identify and analyze certain areas of efficiency and effectiveness within the organization. Assuming management identifies areas for improvement that can be remedied by creating various digital applications, an assessment of culture will aid in determining an acceptable pace for such changes. An internal business climate that is somewhat resistant to or slow to embrace change presents a different set of circumstances than does one that expects and embraces it.

Formulating Digital Strategy   Culture plays an important role in the formulation of an organization's online strategy as well. Understanding that a digital strategy represents an organization's plan for reaching its objectives using digital tactics, management must be aware of a culture's values and beliefs. An organization's digital strategy must blend well with an organization's belief systems in order for the strategy to receive acceptance and support throughout the organization. No vision for an organization can be realized unless members of the organization are supportive and involved.

Implementing Digital Strategy   When an organization reaches the point of putting a digital strategy into action—implementation—its culture will dictate a variety of factors. Most importantly, implementation will most likely involve wholesale change and innovation. An organization's culture determines how open its members are to change and dictates how flexible they are to it. And this will ultimately dictate how *fast* implementation will occur. Given the scenario that change threatens organizational members instead of invigorating them, management may spend more time advocating implementation than actually carrying out the implementation. Management must also consider that all change presents some level of stress to an organization. Such stress can be made positive rather than negative by associating aspects of implementation with certain organizational rituals. Implementation might even call for the creation of new rituals designed to recognize the positive attributes of those involved and reinforce the potential benefits of the process to all stakeholders.

Controlling Digital Dimensioning   After the organization's online strategy has been implemented, management must analyze its effects upon culture. Management must take stock of the changes that the process has created within the organization and question its effects. Has one particular step in the digital dimensioning process created negative by-products, or has its impact been primarily positive and encouraging? Has the process identified individuals who are sources of particularly negative or positive influence? Managers must ask these and other questions of its culture when evaluating the degree of success concerning the effects of the digital dimensioning process upon the organization.

Back to Hewlett-Packard

This section illustrates how digital dimensioning principles apply to true organizational situations. Consider the following information as digital dimensioning advice that a consultant might have given HP management as input for building a healthy and appropriate organizational culture.

"As management at Hewlett-Packard, take seriously the implications of your organization's corporate culture. Culture certainly plays a vital role in building the job satisfaction of your employees and retaining them for the future. It's important to build a healthy culture in an effort to foster creativity and innovation and avoid the costly by-products of employee attrition.

"In analyzing your culture, pay close attention to the issues of language, belief systems, and rituals. By examining the roles they each play and the effects they have had or currently have on the organization, seek to reinforce them, modify them, omit them, or create new ones. In doing so, consider employee empowerment and job enrichment by allowing employees to participate in the process as a whole.

"Culture in the new economy is a much different animal than it was in the old economy. Be sure to monitor the trends and developments in this area as carefully as you do those in technology and industry. Culture can become an organizational barrier or ally. Avoiding the former is a function of strong leadership and management."

Digital Dimensioning Resolutions

- Understand the issue of culture as a fundamental issue within all types of people systems.

- Recognize the importance of language, belief systems, and rituals within cultures.

- Appreciate the enabling role that culture has upon the digital dimensioning process.

- Ensure that management and leadership display behaviors consistent with a healthy culture.

- Analyze the symptoms of positive and negative culture to learn more about your organization's cultural health.

- Stay abreast of cultural trends as routinely as you do those in technology or your industry.

- Analyze cultural issues within acquisition targets or external digital experts.

Appendix A

Survey for Improving Analysis of the Digital Environment (Online Version)

Directions:You are an important part of the decision-making process for determining the digital focus of our organization. As you know, to help you make the best possible impact on this decision-making process, management periodically distributes information analyzing various vital components of our digital environment.

Below are a number of questions about this information that you receive. For most questions, simply click on the number that best represents your opinion. For questions asking for your comments, please key in your opinions.

*When you've finished your survey, click on the **Send Results** button at the end of the survey. Your opinions will be completely anonymous.*

Thanks for your thoughtful participation. Your opinions will undoubtedly help improve how we analyze our digital environment.

Copyrighted by Dr. Samuel C. Certo and Matthew W. Certo. Cannot be used without permission.

Concerning Customers

	Very little	Little	Some	Much	Very much
1. How much information about **customers** have you <u>received</u> from our analysis of the digital environment?	❏	❏	❏	❏	❏
2. How much information about **customers** do you <u>need</u> from our analysis of the digital environment?	❏	❏	❏	❏	❏
3. How much importance do you place on getting this information about **customers**?	❏	❏	❏	❏	❏

4. COMMENTS: Describe any additional information about **customers** that you would like to have as input for making future decisions about our digital activities.

_____

_____

_____

Concerning Technology

	Very little	Little	Some	Much	Very much
5. How much information about **technology** have you <u>received</u> from our analysis of the digital environment?	❏	❏	❏	❏	❏
6. How much information about **technology** do you <u>need</u> from our analysis of the digital environment?	❏	❏	❏	❏	❏
7. How much importance do you place on getting this information about **technology**?	❏	❏	❏	❏	❏

8. COMMENTS: Describe any additional information about **technology** that you would like to have as input for making future decisions about our digital activities.

_____

_____

_____

Concerning Competitors

	Very little	Little	Some	Much	Very much
9. How much information about **competitors** have you <u>received</u> from our analysis of the digital environment?	❏	❏	❏	❏	❏
10. How much information about **competitors** do you <u>need</u> from our analysis of the digital environment?	❏	❏	❏	❏	❏

11. How much importance do you place on
    getting this information about **competitors**?   ❏   ❏   ❏   ❏   ❏

12. COMMENTS: Describe any additional information about **competitors** that you would like to
    have as input for making future decisions about our digital activities.

    _____

    _____

    _____

Concerning Suppliers

	Very little	Little	Some	Much	Very much
13. How much information about **suppliers** have you <u>received</u> from our analysis of the digital environment?	❏	❏	❏	❏	❏
14. How much information about **suppliers** do you <u>need</u> from our analysis of the digital environment?	❏	❏	❏	❏	❏
15. How much importance do you place on getting this information about **suppliers**?	❏	❏	❏	❏	❏

16. COMMENTS: Describe any additional information about **suppliers** that you would like to have
    as input for making future decisions about our digital activities.

    _____

    _____

    _____

Concerning Labor for Performing Digital Activities

	Very little	Little	Some	Much	Very much
17. How much information about **labor** have you <u>received</u> from our analysis of the digital environment?	❏	❏	❏	❏	❏
18. How much information about **labor** do you <u>need</u> from our analysis of the digital environment?	❏	❏	❏	❏	❏
19. How much importance do you place on getting this information about **labor**?	❏	❏	❏	❏	❏

20. COMMENTS: In the space below, describe any additional information that you would like to
    have about **labor** as input for maintaining our digital direction.

    _____

    _____

    _____

Concerning Global Issues Impacting Digital Dimensioning

	Very little	Little	Some	Much	Very much
21. How much information about **global issues** have you <u>received</u> from our analysis of the digital environment?	❑	❑	❑	❑	❑
22. How much information about **global issues** do you <u>need</u> from our analysis of digital environment?	❑	❑	❑	❑	❑
23. How much importance do you place on getting this information about **global issues**?	❑	❑	❑	❑	❑

24. COMMENTS: Describe any additional information about **global issues** that you would like to have as input for making future decisions about our digital activities.

_____

_____

_____

Concerning Social Trends

	Very little	Little	Some	Much	Very much
25. How much information about **social trends** have you <u>received</u> from our analysis of the digital environment?	❑	❑	❑	❑	❑
26. How much information about **social trends** do you <u>need</u> from our analysis of the digital environment?	❑	❑	❑	❑	❑
27. How much importance do you place on getting this information about **social trends**?	❑	❑	❑	❑	❑

28. COMMENTS: Describe any additional information about **social trends** that you would like to have as input for making future decisions about our digital activities.

_____

_____

_____

Concerning Political Trends

	Very little	Little	Some	Much	Very much
29. How much information about **political trends** have you <u>received</u> from our analysis of the digital environment?	❑	❑	❑	❑	❑
30. How much information about **political trends** do you <u>need</u> from our analysis of the digital environment?	❑	❑	❑	❑	❑

31. How much importance do you place on
getting this information about **political trends**? ❏   ❏   ❏   ❏   ❏

32. COMMENTS: Describe any additional information about **political trends** that you would like
to have as input for making future decisions about our digital activities.

_____

_____

_____

Concerning Economic Trends

	Very little	Little	Some	Much	Very much
33. How much information about **economic trends** have you <u>received</u> from our analysis of the digital environment?	❏	❏	❏	❏	❏
34. How much information about **economic trends** do you <u>need</u> from our analysis of the digital environment?	❏	❏	❏	❏	❏
35. How much importance do you place on getting this information about **economic trends**?	❏	❏	❏	❏	❏

36. COMMENTS: Describe any additional information about **economic trends** that you would
like to have as input for making future decisions about our digital activities.

_____

_____

_____

Concerning Legal Issues

	Very little	Little	Some	Much	Very much
37. How much information about **legal issues** have you <u>received</u> from our analysis of the digital environment?	❏	❏	❏	❏	❏
38. How much information about **legal issues** do you <u>need</u> from our analysis of the digital environment?	❏	❏	❏	❏	❏
39. How much importance do you place on getting this information about **legal issues**?	❏	❏	❏	❏	❏

40. COMMENTS: Describe any additional information about **legal issues** that you would like to
have as input for making future decisions about our digital activities.

_____

_____

_____

Concerning Internal Management Issues

	Very little	Little	Some	Much	Very much
41. How much information about **internal management issues** have you <u>received</u> from our analysis of the digital environment?	❑	❑	❑	❑	❑
42. How much information about **internal management issues** do you <u>need</u> from our analysis of the digital environment?	❑	❑	❑	❑	❑
43. How much importance do you place on getting this information about **internal management issues**?	❑	❑	❑	❑	❑

44. COMMENTS: Describe any additional information about **internal management issues** that you would like to have as input for making future decisions about our digital activities.

_____

_____

_____

Concerning Internal Marketing Issues

	Very little	Little	Some	Much	Very much
45. How much information about **internal marketing issues** have you <u>received</u> from our analysis of the digital environment?	❑	❑	❑	❑	❑
46. How much information about **internal marketing issues** do you <u>need</u> from our analysis of the digital environment?	❑	❑	❑	❑	❑
47. How much importance do you place on getting this information about **internal marketing issues**?	❑	❑	❑	❑	❑

48. COMMENTS: Describe any additional information about **internal marketing issues** that you would like to have as input for making future decisions about our digital activities.

_____

_____

_____

Concerning Internal Finance Issues

	Very little	Little	Some	Much	Very much
49. How much information about **internal finance issues** have you <u>received</u> from our analysis of te digital environment?	❑	❑	❑	❑	❑
50. How much information about **internal finance issues** do you <u>need</u> from our analysis of the digital environment?	❑	❑	❑	❑	❑

51. How much importance do you place on getting
this information about **internal finance issues**? ❑   ❑   ❑   ❑   ❑

52. COMMENTS: Describe any additional information about **internal finance issues** that you
would like to have as input for making future decisions about our digital activities.

_____

_____

_____

Concerning Internal Human Resource Issues

	Very little	Little	Some	Much	Very much
53. How much information about **internal human resource issues** have you <u>received</u> from our analysis of the digital environment?	❑	❑	❑	❑	❑
54. How much information about **internal human resource issues** do you <u>need</u> from our analysis of the digital environment?	❑	❑	❑	❑	❑
55. How much importance do you place on getting this information about **internal human resource issues**?	❑	❑	❑	❑	❑

56. COMMENTS: Describe any additional information about **internal human resource issues**
that you would like to have as input for making future decisions about our digital activities.

_____

_____

_____

Concerning Internal Operations Issues

	Very little	Little	Some	Much	Very much
57. How much information about **internal operations issues** have you <u>received</u> from our analysis of the digital environment?	❑	❑	❑	❑	❑
58. How much information about **internal operations issues** do you <u>need</u> from our analysis of the digital environment?	❑	❑	❑	❑	❑
59. How much importance do you place on getting this information about **internal operating issues**?	❑	❑	❑	❑	❑

60. COMMENTS: In the space below, describe any additional information that you would like to
have about **internal operating issues** as input for maintaining our digital direction.

_____

_____

_____

Concerning Existing Digital Presence

	Very little	Little	Some	Much	Very much
61. How much information about **existing digital presence** have you <u>received</u> from our analysis of the digital environment?	❏	❏	❏	❏	❏
62. How much information about **existing digital presence** do you <u>need</u> from our analysis of the digital environment?	❏	❏	❏	❏	❏
63. How much importance do you place on getting this information about **existing digital presence**?	❏	❏	❏	❏	❏

64. COMMENTS: Describe any additional information about **existing digital presence** that you would like to have as input for making future decisions about our digital activities.

_____

_____

_____

Send Results

Appendix B

Survey for Improving Digital Support (Online Version)

Directions: As you know, our company carries out many digital activities aimed at helping us to reach our goals. These activities allocate digital support to marketing, operations, human resources, and the rest of our functions.

The purpose of this survey is to determine the overall value of the digital support activities that we currently perform. To what extent are these activities actually helpful (effective) in achieving our goals? To what extent are the activities wasteful (inefficient)?

Below are a number of questions about the digital support activities that we perform. For most questions, simply click on the number that best represents your opinion. For questions asking for your comments, please key in your opinions.

*When you've finished, click on the **Send Results** button at the end of the survey. Your opinions will be completely anonymous.*

Thanks for your thoughtful participation. Your opinions will certainly help to improve the overall usefulness of our digital support activities.

Copyrighted by Dr. Samuel C. Certo and Matthew W. Certo. Cannot be used without permission.

Concerning Marketing

	Very little	Little	Some	Much	Very much
1. How much do digital activities aimed at supporting **marketing** actually contribute to reaching **marketing** goals?	❏	❏	❏	❏	❏
2. How much waste (inefficiency) is involved in performing these activities?	❏	❏	❏	❏	❏

3. COMMENTS: How can we make digital activities more useful in reaching **marketing** goals? _____

_____

_____

_____

4. COMMENTS: How can we make digital activities that support **marketing** less wasteful (more efficient)? _____

_____

_____

_____

Concerning Human Resources

	Very little	Little	Some	Much	Very much
5. How much do our digital activities aimed at supporting **human resources** actually contribute to reaching our **human resources** goals?	❏	❏	❏	❏	❏
6. How much waste (inefficiency) is involved in performing these activities?	❏	❏	❏	❏	❏

7. COMMENTS: What are your ideas for making digital activities more useful in reaching **human resources** goals?_____

_____

_____

_____

8. COMMENTS: What are your ideas for making digital activities that support **human resources** less wasteful (more efficient)? _____

_____

_____

_____

Concerning Sales

	Very little	Little	Some	Much	Very much
9. How much do our digital activities aimed at supporting **sales** actually contribute to reaching our **sales** goals?	❏	❏	❏	❏	❏
10. How much waste (inefficiency) is involved in performing these activities?	❏	❏	❏	❏	❏

11. COMMENTS: What are your ideas for making digital activities more useful in reaching **sales** goals? _____

_____

_____

_____

12. COMMENTS: What are your ideas for making digital activities that support **sales** less wasteful (more efficient)? _____

_____

_____

_____

Concerning Operations

	Very little	Little	Some	Much	Very much
13. How much do our digital activities aimed at supporting **operations** actually contribute to reaching our **operations** goals?	❏	❏	❏	❏	❏
14. How much waste (inefficiency) is involved in performing these activities?	❏	❏	❏	❏	❏

15. COMMENTS: What are your ideas for making digital activities more useful in reaching **operations** goals? _____

_____

_____

_____

16. COMMENTS: What are your ideas for making digital activities that support **operations** less wasteful (more efficient)? _____

_____

_____

_____

Concerning Internal Communication

	Very little	Little	Some	Much	Very much
17. How much do our digital activities aimed at supporting **internal communication** actually contribute to reaching our **internal communication** goals?	❏	❏	❏	❏	❏
18. How much waste (inefficiency) is involved in performing these activities?	❏	❏	❏	❏	❏

19. COMMENTS: What are your ideas for making digital activities more useful in reaching **internal communication** goals? _____

_____

_____

_____

20. COMMENTS: What are your ideas for making digital activities that support **internal communication** less wasteful (more efficient)? _____

_____

_____

_____

Concerning Innovation

	Very little	Little	Some	Much	Very much
21. How much do our digital activities aimed at supporting **innovation** actually contribute to reaching our **innovation** goals?	❏	❏	❏	❏	❏
22. How much waste (inefficiency) is involved in performing these activities?	❏	❏	❏	❏	❏

23. COMMENTS: What are your ideas for making digital activities more useful in reaching **innovation** goals? _____

_____

_____

_____

24. COMMENTS: What are your ideas for making digital activities that support **innovation** less wasteful (more efficient)? _____

_____

_____

_____

Concerning Productivity

	Very little	Little	Some	Much	Very much
25. How much do our digital activities aimed at supporting **productivity** actually contribute to reaching our **productivity** goals?	❏	❏	❏	❏	❏
26. How much waste (inefficiency) is involved in performing these activities?	❏	❏	❏	❏	❏

27. COMMENTS: What are your ideas for making digital activities more useful in reaching **productivity** goals? _____

_____

_____

_____

28. COMMENTS: What are your ideas for making digital activities that support **productivity** less wasteful (more efficient)? _____

_____

_____

_____

Concerning Social Responsibility

	Very little	Little	Some	Much	Very much
29. How much do our digital activities aimed at supporting **social responsibility** actually contribute to reaching our **social responsibility** goals?	❏	❏	❏	❏	❏
30. How much waste (inefficiency) is involved in performing these activities?	❏	❏	❏	❏	❏

31. What are your ideas for making digital activities more useful in reaching **social responsibility** goals? _____

_____

_____

_____

32. What are your ideas for making digital activities that support **social responsibility** less wasteful (more efficient)? _____

_____

_____

_____

Concerning Profitability

	Very little	Little	Some	Much	Very much
33. How much do our digital activities aimed at supporting **profitability** actually contribute to reaching our **profitability** goals?	❏	❏	❏	❏	❏
34. How much waste (inefficiency is involved in performing these activities?	❏	❏	❏	❏	❏

35. COMMENTS: What are your ideas for making digital activities more useful in reaching **profitability** goals? _____
_____
_____
_____

36. COMMENTS: What are your ideas for making digital activities that support **profitability** less wasteful (more efficient)? _____
_____
_____
_____

Send Results

References

Chapter 2

1. This Spotlight is based upon Bob Violino, "Office Depot builds winning strategy on the Web," *Informationweek*, no. 765, Dec. 13, 1999, pp. 84–86.

2. Denise Worach, "Online billing: Savings oversold?" *Public Utilities Fortnightly*, Spring 2000, pp. 32–40.

3. Myra Pinkham, "Ryerson Tull tries dual e-business strategy," *Metal Center News*, Vol. 40, no. 9, August 2000, pp. 50–54.

4. Robert Preston and Rutrell Yasin, "Transformation isn't easy— Dow's new chemistry,", *Internetweek*, no. 822, July 24, 2000, p. 1, 54ff.

5. Steve Konicki, "Fork in e-biz expressway?" *Informationweek*, no. 799, no. 799, Aug. 14, 2000, pp. 22–24.

6. Cora Daniels, "The trauma of rebirth," *Fortune*, vol. 142, no. 5, Sept. 4, 2000, pp. 367–374.

7. Samuel C. Certo and J. Paul Peter, *The Strategic Management Process* (Irwin/Austen Press, Chicago, 1995).

8. Samuel C. Certo, *Modern Management* (Prentice Hall, Upper Saddle River, NJ, 2000) 8th ed.

9. Kenneth J. Rose and James A. Hendricks, "Accountants overseas," *Management Accounting*, vol. 80, no. 7, January 1999, pp. 34–38.

10. Lori Jacobson, "Shop, click, send," *Potentials*, vol. 32, no. 11, November 1999, p. 6.

11. Shari Weiss, "Drinks recipes drive visitors to Friday's' Internet links," *Nation's Restaurant News*, vol. 34, no. 34, Aug. 21, 2000, p. 34.

Chapter 4

1. This Spotlight based upon Frank N. Wilner. "Is a web-centric approach the way to go?" *Railway Age*, vol. 201, no. 7, July 2000, p. 76; and Marc J. Epstein, "Organizing your business for the Internet evolution," *Strategic Finance*, vol. 82, no. 1, July 2000, pp. 56–60.

Chapter 5

1. This Spotlight is based upon John Teresko, "Remaking the automakers," *Industry Week*, vol. 248, no. 18, Oct. 4, 1999, pp. 40–44; and Alex Taylor III, "Ralph's Agenda," *eCompany*, July 2000, pp. 97–101.

2. George V. Hulme, "Premium put on Web initiatives," *Informationweek*, no. 803, Sept. 11, 2000, p. 289.

3. Anna Bernasek, "Pattern for prosperity," *Fortune*, vol. 142, no. 7, Oct. 2, 2000, pp. 100–108.

Chapter 6

1. This spotlight is based upon Karen Mazurkewich, "Ready for take-off," *Far Eastern Economic Review*, vol. 163, no. 39, Sept. 28, 2000, p. 43; and John Evan Frook, "From The Top," *Internetweek*, no. 732, Sept. 14, 1998, p 22.

2. Richard Karpinski, "The right stuff for Boeing's extranet—Business unit slashes costs to woo back customers from cutthroat competitor," *Internetweek*, no. 756, Mar. 15, 1999, p 9.

3. *Cisco Systems Annual Report*, 2000, p. 12.

4. Scott Parker, "Becoming a strategic e-business partner," *Corporate Finance*, September 2000, pp. 2–4.

5. John Dalton, "Internet marketing to physicians creating footprint for providers," *Health Industry Today*, vol. 62, no. 9, September 1999, pp. 1, 8+.

6. "Lands' End introduces new collaborative shopping aids," *Direct Marketing*, vol. 62, no. 7, November 1999, p. 15.

7. Matt Hamblen, "Shell protects brand via net," *Computerworld*, vol. 34, no. 2, Jan. 10, 2000, p. 39.

8. Luisa Kroll, "Good morning, HAL," *Forbes*, vol. 163, no. 5, Mar. 8, 1999, pp. 118-120.

9. Michael Porter, *Competitive Advantage* (Free Press, New York, 1985).

10. Susan Reda, "Winn-Dixie cuts utility costs with Internet-based data network," *Stores*, vol. 81, no. 9, September 1999, pp. 163-165.

11. J. William Gurley, "A Dell for every industry," *Fortune*, vol. 138, no. 7, Oct. 12, 1998, pp. 167-172.

12. Craig Addison, "Intel's Taiwan connection," *Electronic Business*, October 1999, pp. s24-s25.

13. Mitch Wagner, "Hilton's online strategy nets four-star rating—Hotel chain uses Internet to increase sales, link to customers and cut procurement costs," *Internetweek*, no. 817, June 12, 2000, pp. 89-90.

Chapter 7

1. This Spotlight is based upon Ram Charan, *Informationweek Online*, Nov. 1, 1999.

Chapter 8

1. This Spotlight is based upon Marianne Kolbasuk McGee, "Lessons from a cultural revolution," *Informationweek*, no. 758, Oct. 25, 1999, pp. 46-62.

2. Samuel C. Certo, *Modern Management* (Prentice Hall, Upper Saddle River, NJ, 2000), p. 422.

3. Jaikumar Vijayan, "Caught in the middle", *Computerworld*, vol. 34, no. 30, July 24, 2000, pp. 70-71; Susan Strother Clarke, "OurBeginning changes dot-com game plan," *Orlando Sentinel*, Dec. 8, 2000, pp. C1, C6.

4. J. P. Donlon, "Big brown boots up," *Chief Executive*, no. 142, March 1999, pp. 30-36.

5. Debbie Howell, "Garden.com folds for lack of funds," *Retailing Today*, vol. 39, no. 23, Dec. 11, 2000, p. 10.

6. Jerry Jackson, "Olivegarden.com helps unravel mystery of wine," *Orlando Sentinel CFB*, Dec. 18–24, 2000, p. 3.

7. Marianne Kolbasuk McGee, "Wake-up call," *Informationweek*, no. 804, Sept. 18, 2000, pp. 55–65.

8. Susan Caminiti, "Toys 'R' Us scoots back to the Web," *Corporate Board Member*, vol. 3, no. 4, Winter 2000, pp. 30–36.

9. Matt Krantz, "What detonated the dot-bombs?" *USA Today*, Dec. 4, 2000, pp. 1B, 2B.

10. L. Scott Tillett, "It's back from the dead: Boo.com," *Internetweek*, no. 834, Oct. 23, 2000, p. 11.

Chapter 9

1. This Spotlight is based on *The Economist*, July 15, 2000, pp. 59–60

2. Robert Goffee, *Character of a Corporation* (Harper Business, New York, 1998), p. 9.

3. Robert Goffee, *Character of a Corporation*, p. 15

4. Bart Ziegler, *Wall Street Journal*, Feb. 3, 1995.

5. David L. Stum, *HR Focus*, New York, September 1998.

6. *Wired*, December 2000.

7. Stacy Cowley, *Silicon Alley Daily*, Oct. 19, 1999.

Glossary

After-control—Digital dimensioning control that takes place after digital dimensioning activities are performed.

Analyzing the digital environment—Monitoring an organization's digital surroundings to identify strengths, weaknesses, opportunities, and threats serving as a foundation for determining an organization's digital direction.

Before-control—Digital dimensioning control that takes place before digital activities are performed.

Belief system—Collection of shared values or ideals within a culture

Business operations—Activities supporting an organization or business unit(s) that operates primarily within a single industry.

Combined cost curve—The trend of cash outflow that comprises start-up and operational expenses.

Competitor component—The component of the operating level of the organization's digital environment that focuses on rivals that an organization must overcome in order to reach its objectives.

Comprehensive digital strategy—Digital strategy that addresses a significant proportion of the digital opportunities available to an organization.

Conceptual skill—The ability to see the organization as a whole and design ebusiness activities to suit that view.

Control—Making something happen the way it was planned to happen.

Controlling—The process of making sure that events occur as planned.

Corporate culture—Belief systems, values, and rules within an organizational or corporate setting.

Corporate operations—Activities that support the management of a complex corporation as a whole.

Cost-benefit—The process of comparing the cost of an activity with the benefit or return of performing the activity.

Cost leadership—A philosophy that focuses on achieving competitive advantage and, as a result, organizational success by gaining acceptable returns through the minimization of costs.

Critical question measurement—A digital audit measurement technique involving the formulation of important questions regarding the digital dimensioning activities of an organization, the answers to those questions, and the evaluation of the answers.

Culture—The mortarlike bond between people in a people system which guides how they talk, work, dress, celebrate, and perform any other activity that might be relevant to their existence.

Customer component—The component of the operating level of the organization's digital environment that focuses on the characteristics and behavior of those who buy the organization's goods and services.

Differentiation—A philosophy that focuses on marketing unique products that will sell for premium prices.

Digital—A descriptor referring to the Internet as well as other Internet-enhancing electronic technologies.

Digital audit—An examination of an organization's digital dimensioning activities.

Digital component—The segment of the internal level of an organization's digital environment that houses factors related to the digital condition of the organization.

Digital dimensioning—The process of crafting some combination of Internet and supportive electronic technologies to solve business problems and thus help organizations reach their goals.

Digital dimensioning control—A special type of organizational control that focuses on monitoring and evaluating the digital dimensioning process to ensure that expected digital results are achieved.

Digital dimensioning risk—The chance of loss of resources invested in digital dimensioning activities.

Digital direction—An organization's broad digital thrust that is consistent with the accomplishment of organizational purpose.

Digital environment—The set of factors, both outside and inside the organization, that can affect digital performance.

Digital expertise—Those human resources with the appropriate skills required to participate in the digital dimensioning process.

Digital implementation—The process of putting digital strategy into action.

Digital standards—Acceptable levels of digital results that reflect digital support goals, and serve as yardsticks for evaluating digital performance.

Digital strategy—An organization's master plan that outlines how digital activities will support its statement of digital direction, digital support goals, and, ultimately, organizational success.

Digital support effectiveness—The degree to which digital efforts actually help an organization to reach established goals.

Digital support efficiency—The proportion of resources allocated to performing digital activities that finally contributes to reaching established goals.

Digital support goals—Targets that, when reached, aid the attainment of established organizational goals and thereby help fulfill organizational purpose.

Digital support grid—A matrix that considers both effectiveness and efficiency in determining the overall impact of digital support activities.

Digital tactics—Maneuvers for enhancing the probability that digital strategy will be successful.

Dimensioning—The process of crafting some object or entity with calculated intent.

Diversification—A philosophy that emphasizes building an organization by operating in two or more different industries or with two or more different lines of business.

During-control—Digital dimensioning control that takes place while digital dimensioning activities are being performed.

Ebusiness cultivators—commercial internet Initiatives which show promise toward positive earnings growth, positive cash flow, and increased shareholder value

Ebusiness defenders—Financially struggling Internet initiatives forced to assume defensive positions to continue operations.

Ebusiness failures—Commercial Internet initiatives that are terminated due to improperly managed finances or growth.

Ebusiness successes—Those organizations that display trends of positive earnings growth, positive cashflow, and increased shareholder value.

Economic component—The component of the general level of an organization's digital environment that focuses on the distribution and uses of resources within an entire society.

Empowerment—Management function that places authority or responsibility within individual employees.

Execution—The process of putting the implementation plan into action.

External expertise—Outside consultants and vendors that possess digital expertise available to supplement internal expertise.

Finance component—The segment of the internal level of an organization's digital environment that consists of factors related to the financial condition of the organization.

Focus—A philosophy that emphasizes gaining competitive advantage by segmenting markets and appealing to only one or a few select groups of consumers or organizational buyers.

Formulating digital strategy—Actually developing digital strategy.

General level—The level of an organization's digital environment that is outside the organization, has components that are relatively slow in changing, and tends to impact digital direction relatively slowly over time.

Horizontal integration—A philosophy that emphasizes growing an organization by acquiring competing firms in the same line of business.

Human resource component—The segment of the internal level of an organization's digital environment that entails factors related to managing human resources within the organization.

Human resource management—The organizational function that focuses on providing appropriate human resources for the organization.

Implementation companies—Resources of external expertise specializing in the implementation of third-party software systems.

Implementation plan—Tangible document that is the end product of implementation planning.

Implementation planning—The process of scheduling and prioritizing implementation activities.

Implementation scheduling—The process of establishing a timetable for the design, development, testing, and launch of digital applications.

Improving digital activities—Modifying digital dimensioning activities to ensure that they better meet digital standards and thereby better contribute to reaching digital support goals.

Influencing—The process of guiding the activities of people in appropriate directions.

Innovation goal—Organizational target stipulating management's commitment to finding new, better methods of conducting organizational business.

Insolvency—Economic term for depleted or bankrupt financial resources.

Interactive agencies—Resources of external expertise specializing in online branding, advertising, and marketing.

Internal business unit—Separate business unit incubated by the parent company to focus on specific commercial opportunities.

Internal expertise—Those employees of an organization who possess digital expertise.

Internal level—The level of the organization's digital environment that is inside the organization, has components that tend to change quickly, and tends to impact digital direction quickly.

Labor component—The component of the operating level of the organization's digital environment that focuses on influences on the supply of workers available to perform needed organizational tasks.

Language—The manner of speaking or communicating used within a culture.

Legal component—The component of the general level of the organization's digital environment that consists of laws that members of society are expected to follow.

Management component—The component of the internal level of an organization's digital environment that consists of all the factors dealing with planning, organizing, influencing, and controlling.

Management consulting firms—Resources of external expertise specializing in the areas of conceptual strategy and implementation.

Marketing—The organizational function that facilitates the exchange of goods and services between an organization and its customers.

Marketing component—The segment of the internal level of an organization's digital environment that contains factors relating to selling goods and services to customers.

Murphy's law—A lighthearted axiom saying that anything that can go wrong will go wrong.

Negative culture—Culture in which the variables of language, beliefs, and ritual create adverse circumstances for employees.

Online retailers—Electronic retail storefronts that receive orders via the Internet and ship products to consumers through various shipping partners.

Operating level—The level of the organization's digital environment that is outside the organization, has components that are relatively quick in changing, and tends to impact digital direction relatively quickly.

Operational digital support goal—A digital support goal stated in such a way that an attempt to attain it can be measured and compared with the goal itself to determine whether it actually has been attained.

Operational expenses—Those ongoing expenses necessary to a company's continuing operations.

Operations—The organizational function that produces an organization's goods and services.

Operations component—The segment of the internal level of an organization's digital environment that consists of all factors dealing with the organizational process used to produce goods and services.

Organizational function—A major activity performed within an organization.

Organizing—The process of establishing orderly uses for all resources within an organization.

People skill—The ability to influence stakeholders to become focused on and involved in carrying out ebusiness activities.

People system—Any community of individuals living, working, and/or operating together.

Planning—The process of establishing organizational goals, choosing tasks that must be done in order to reach those goals, outlining how the tasks should be performed, and determining when the tasks should be performed.

Political component—The component of the general level of an organization's digital environment that relates to government affairs.

Positive culture—Culture in which the variables of language, beliefs, and ritual create favorable circumstances for employees.

Productivity—The level of an organization's output in relation to the resources needed to produce the output.

Productivity goal—Organizational target stipulating the level of productivity that an organization is striving to reach.

Profit goal—organizational target stipulating how much excess of revenue over cost that management would like to retain.

Research and development—The organizational function for generating a steady stream of new products and processes.

Resource allocation—The planning and distribution of those resources necessary for successful digital implementation.

Ritual—Ceremony or act designed to reinforce a belief system or memorialize an event or milestone.

Skill availability—A measure of how accessible and dedicated internal expertise can be with regard to the digital dimensioning process.

Skill level—The degree of skill that a digital expert possesses.

Social component—The component of the general level of an organization's digital environment that describes characteristics of the society or societies in which the organization exists.

Social responsibility—The obligation of business to help improve the welfare of society while it strives to reach other organizational goals.

Social responsibility goal—Organizational target that, when achieved, will not only contribute to the success of the organization, but contribute to the general welfare of society.

Spin-off—A subsidiary company formed to operate separately from its parent.

Stakeholders—People who are interested in an organization because they are significantly affected by the organization's success or failure.

Start-up expenses—One-time expenses necessary to establishing operational infrastructure and setting up operations.

Statement of digital direction—A statement expressing how digital activities in an organization will be focused in order to help accomplish organizational purpose.

Strategic management—Long-range planning that focuses on moving the organization as a whole toward achieving established organizational goals in about 3 to 5 years.

Supplier component—The component of the operating level of the organization's digital environment that focuses on the influence of providers of resources to the organization.

Survey for Evaluating Digital Environment Analysis—A questionnaire that managers can use to determine if enough information is being gathered for digital environment analysis, to decide if the information gathered is valuable, and to pinpoint new information needed to improve the analysis.

Survey measurement—A digital audit method for measuring digital performance through the design and administration of specially focused surveys.

SWOT analysis—A technique for transforming the complex body of information generated from the analysis of the digital environment into a simple pattern that enhances both understanding and appropriate reaction to the digital environment.

Systems providers—Resources of external expertise which provide hardware, software, and installation services to organizations.

Technical skill—The ability to use ebusiness hardware and software.

Technology component—The component of the operating level of the organization's digital environment that focuses on new approaches to producing goods and services: new business methods as well as new equipment.

Traditional retailers—Retail stores that have physical locations at which customers purchase goods.

Vertical integration—A philosophy that emphasizes growing an organization by adding functions previously performed by a supplier or distributor.

Index

About the Authors

Samuel C. Certo, Ph.D., is a cofounder of WebSolvers, Inc., a consultancy specializing in developing ebusiness solutions for corporations. The author of several successful college textbooks, Dr. Certo is a former dean and presently a professor of management at the Crummer Graduate School of Business at Rollins College.

Matthew W. Certo is cofounder, president, and chief executive officer of WebSolvers. In 1999, he was honored with the Orlando Business Journal "40 Under 40" distinction for demonstrating success and achievement in commerce, leadership, and community involvement.